100 MORE THINGS

YOU DON'T NEED A MAN FOR!

Exterior Home and Garden Maintenance

100 MORE THINGS

YOU DON'T NEED A MAN FOR!

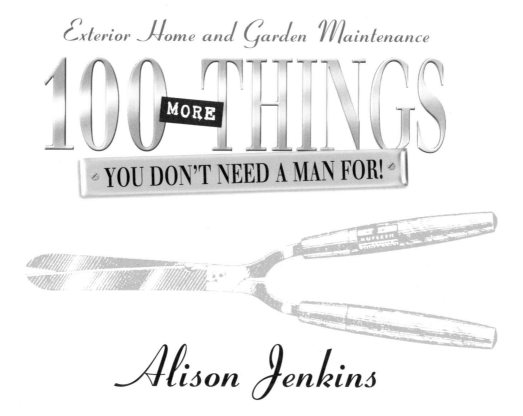

Alison Jenkins

TED SMART

This edition produced in 2003 for

THE BOOK PEOPLE LTD

Hall Wood Avenue

Haydock

St. Helens WA11 9UL

This book was conceived, designed and produced by

THE IVY PRESS LIMITED

The Old Candlemakers, West Street

Lewes, East Sussex BN7 2NZ

Creative Director: PETER BRIDGEWATER
Publisher: SOPHIE COLLINS
Editorial Director: STEVE LUCK
Art Director: CLARE BARBER
Designer: KEVIN KNIGHT
Mac Design: GINNY ZEAL
Senior Project Editor: CAROLINE EARLE
Photographer: CALVEY TAYLOR-HAW
Additional Photography: PAUL MANSER
Illustrators: ANNA HUNTER-DOWNING, IVAN HISSEY
Picture Researcher: SHARON DORTENZIO

A catalogue record for this book is available from the British Library

Printed and bound by Hong Kong Graphics and Printing, China

Contents

ANOTHER **100** MAN-FREE ACTIVITIES!

* WHY DON'T WE DO IT IN THE GARDEN?

TIME TO GET YOUR TOOLS OUT AGAIN!

Introduction

HEY, LOOK, MORE HOME IMPROVEMENT, GIRLS – AND THIS TIME WE GET TO PLAY WITH CHAINSAWS!

LET ME AT THAT HEAVY MACHINERY!

MY, LOOK AT THAT LOVELY WHEELBARROW!

IN MY first book, *100 Things You Don't Need a Man For!*, I took a tongue-in-cheek look at interior repairs and decoration from the viewpoint of an eager and enthusiastic first-time (but penniless) home owner — me. Well, the inside is looking lovely now — so what to do next? The great outdoors beckoned, the call of the wild... OK, I just looked out of the window and saw green rambling undergrowth and thought: 'Oh dear! I forgot about the outside.' Everyone says that you should wait a full cycle of seasons before doing anything to the garden so you know what's there, bulbs and stuff like that — but I don't think that applies to mowing the grass!

I don't really intend to talk about gardening here; what I'm talking about is simple repairs and maintenance from the rooftop to the drains, exterior deco-rating and fencing, patios and pathways, outdoor living, decks and diggin' dirt, with a bit of garden taming thrown in for good measure! So let's talk about the exterior — the garden, the yard, call it what you will, your outside space is an extension of the inside and is deserving of as much attention. Your garden should be a space for relaxing and enter-taining, for being at one with nature or barbecuing with your friends! That brings us to the question: 'Why do it yourself?' Well, ladies, if, like me, you have big ideas and a small bank balance, then the answer is crystal-clear — cash! I like to have fun and I also like to shop, so if I can save myself some money on the home-improvement front then I will quite happily do so — more money to spend on shoes! Why spend all your hard-earned cash on hired help if you can do it yourself?

I'VE BEEN SO WORRIED SINCE SHE ASKED FOR A BULLDOZER FOR OUR ANNIVERSARY!

Most basic maintenance and repair tasks are simple; you just need to know how and what to do. This book will tell it like it is, plain and simple — no complicated jargon that'll have your eyes glazed over in a minute, and hopefully you'll have a giggle, too. But, girls, don't forget, the joy of home improvement is knowing how, what and when to do it. It's also about knowing when not to — check out the last section when you find yourself requiring the services of a man who can.

When embarking upon an outdoor DIY task, basic principles apply, so don't forget the two Ps — Preparation Pays! If a job's worth doing, then it is worth doing well; thorough preparation is essential to achieving successful results. Accessories, too, are vital, as every girl knows. Take this opportunity to add to your toolbox (or start one if you haven't got one!), and remember to choose the right tool for the job — matching accessories! Browse at your leisure through the 'Tools Out!' section. Make sure you have all the right stuff to make your home-improvement tasks a cinch.

So, girls, with the aid of this book you'll be fully tooled up, outfitted and ready to go in no time. Anyone know what colour wellies we'll be wearing next season? Enjoy!

Creative project key

☞ How long, how much and how difficult? Use the key below as a guide to the creative projects featured throughout the book.

🔨 very easy to make

🔨🔨 not difficult, some thinking required

🔨🔨🔨 not for the complete beginner

£ unbelievably cheap

££ value for money

£££ not cheap, but cheaper than buying it

☕ finished in no time

☕☕ around half a day's work

☕☕☕ around a day's work

☕☕☕ set aside a whole weekend

❀ HMM... I'M ALWAYS ON THE LOOKOUT FOR AN OUTDOOR PROJECT...

TOOLS OUT!

Here we have lots of wonderful tools for outdoor maintenance. What a shopping opportunity!

Tooling up for the great outdoors

Most indoor home-improvement tools contained in a girl's basic toolbox can be put to equally good use outdoors, too. If you have already got your basic kit together, give yourself a pat on the back and read on smugly! However, if the words 'tool kit' have an unfamiliar ring, don't despair, just peruse the following pages of tools and materials — some essential, some non-essential and some to hire for that one-time-only job. Remember: you don't have to rush to the DIY store and get everything at once; just buy a few essentials first and then add to your collection as and when required.

HAND TOOLS BASIC

'But all tools are hand tools because you use your hands,' I can hear you say. That's true, but what I'm talking about are 'hand' as opposed to 'power' tools. That is, tools that don't run on electricity from either a socket or a battery. You have to use your own elbow grease to work them — the power tools will come later on. These versatile hand tools are just as useful outdoors as they are indoors.

Staple gun
Use this to attach lightweight materials in place, for example fly screening or canvas.

No unpleasant grinding with this — when the blade's blunt, just chuck it!

Hacksaw
You can buy general-purpose and mini hacksaws. Both types of saw cut metal tubes, rods and sheets. Use the big hacksaw for large metal-cutting jobs and the smaller one to cut in constricted areas.

Screwdrivers

You can get a matching set of screwdrivers in any DIY store. You will find flat-head screwdrivers for use with screws with a slotted head, and cross-head (Pozidrive or Phillips) screwdrivers for screws with a cross-shaped indentation in the head.

Pliers

A set of three: long-nosed, flat-nosed and a snippy one called a side-cutter. To grip, bend, squeeze or shape wires or metal.

Stanley knife

Everyone should have a Stanley knife, preferably one with a retractable blade so that it is safe in the tool bag. Use it for general light cutting and scoring, but be careful not to cut yourself.

Locking pliers

This tool holds things together while you work. Use the adjusting screw to vary the opening of the jaws, then squeeze the pliers shut. Press the release lever to loosen it.

Chalk line

Use this little gadget to make a straight line to guide you in getting things lined up.

CAN'T DO WITHOUT

Tenon saw Use this rigid saw for making straight cuts across wood.

Chisel set A set of three (small, medium and large) will suffice. Used in woodwork for paring, trimming and cutting out waste.

Claw hammer This heavy, versatile, general-purpose hammer is a tool-kit 'must have'. The 'claw' at the back of the hammer head is used to lever out nails.

Pin hammer A lightweight tool used to drive in small nails, pins and tacks.

Centre punch This hard metal punch marks the centre of holes to be drilled, in materials such as metal.

Straightedge Keep a long, sturdy metal rule handy for drawing straight lines or for when you are using a Stanley knife to cut something.

Bradawl This is a small tool with a pointed spike, useful for making pilot holes in wood before driving in a screw; good for making holes in other materials, too.

More indoor tools for outdoor use

POWER TOOLS

Now we're talking! Power tools can be the plug-into-the-socket type or the cordless variety that run on an internal rechargeable battery. Either way, power tools are fabulous pieces of equipment and will make your DIY tasks easier.

Electric screwdriver

Yet another of those 'must haves'. A power screwdriver really is the ticket if you've got lots of screws to drive in – or out, because you can unscrew with it, too. Saves getting nasty blisters on your hands.

Drill bits

Start with a set of multi-purpose drill bits – for both wood and masonry – then add to the collection. You should also get a few flat or spade bits, for making larger holes, and a countersink bit, which makes a nice recess so that the screwhead lies flush.

Electric drill

A drill was my very first power-tool purchase and is an absolute essential in my opinion – with a flex or without. Make sure it has variable speeds and a hammer function as an option.

USING ELECTRICITY OUTDOORS SAFELY

☞ When using electrical equipment, it is vital to take the necessary safety precautions, especially when working outdoors. Circuit breakers are handy little devices that you can plug into the mains, and then you plug your tool or extension cable into it. Read the testing and setting instructions provided and follow them carefully. The circuit breaker will automatically trip and cut off the electricity supply immediately if there is an overload in the wiring or something disastrous occurs (for instance, you mow over your lawnmower cable by mistake). It's very important to use one of these whenever you are working with power tools, both indoors and outdoors. Cordless tools are probably the ideal solution in an outdoor situation because they operate on low voltage.

✲ OH, NO, SOMEONE'S TAKEN THE KITCHEN SINK!

Jigsaw

Believe me, a jigsaw is a truly wonderful thing – essential for cutting curves and wiggly lines, but also useful for making fast, straight cuts. Most jigsaws will have an adjustable guide for this purpose, so that you will be able to cut parallel to an edge, for example.

WARNING

☞ Power tools can be dangerous if not used properly and with care. Always read the operating manual before use and make sure that you understand all the instructions.

☞ Always switch off the power supply when changing bits or blades, and make sure these are securely fitted before you start work.

☞ Don't use a power tool with a worn or frayed flex.

☞ Tie your hair back and don't wear very loose clothing while using power tools, to keep anything from getting caught.

Portable workbench

This is not essential, but is extremely useful when working outdoors – a nice portable work surface for sawing on and so on.

Power sander

This is definitely one of those 'can't do without' labour-saving devices. Sanding is laborious and time-consuming, but it is very important to do it properly and thoroughly if you want good results. Anything that saves time and effort gets my vote, so invest in a belt or orbital sander, as well as a detail sander for awkward corners.

Outdoor extension lead

Unless you are fully tooled up with cordless items, you will need an extension lead in order to use your power tools outside. Get a long, heavy-duty, exterior one. Do NOT use one meant for indoor use – this could be dangerous.

AIN'T NOTHING LIKE THE REEL THING, BABY!

What type of tool for the roof?

ROOFING AND CLADDING

GOING UP!

'Help!' I hear you cry, 'this is a job for the big boys.' Don't panic, I'm not talking major roof installation here, just a little repair and maintenance here and there. Any girl worth the name can patch up cracked tiles that are within easy reach. Carrying out minor repairs to roofs and cladding will save you money in the long run — and it's well worth investing in some of these useful tools.

Tin snips
Essential when up on the roof. Try cutting metal, UPVC material or flashing with anything else, and you'll have problems. Remember: always get the right tool for the job.

Plugging chisel
Use one of these to remove all the old, loose mortar when you have a repointing job to do. Place the point in the mortar, then tap the head with a club hammer.

✳ BOY, DOES YOUR ROOF NEED SOME NEW TILES!

Sliding bevel
A gadget that helps you to measure angles accurately so that you can cut your materials to fit neatly.

Putty knife
Use this handy tool for applying and shaping filler.

TOOLS TO HIRE

Power circular saw You may need one of these for cutting cladding and other materials. It is also possible to cut masonry materials with it, but you'll need a diamond blade for this. Best to hire one, because you'll probably only need to use it once in a while.

Goggles and mask

Wear these when handling or cutting abrasive materials. They don't look very gorgeous, but better safe than sorry.

MORE

ESSENTIALS

Ladder You'll never get up on the roof without one of these. See pages 18–19 for further information.

Chalk line This gadget will make a straight line to guide you in getting things lined up (*see also page 11*).

Steel tape You need this for measuring – especially for measuring long distances.

Screwdrivers Borrow these from your general toolbox to help you get those screws in and out.

Caulking (filling) gun Handy if you have a lot of filling to do. You can use a putty knife and filling compound, but it'll take longer and be more messy.

Claw hammer To prise out all the old nails and bang in those nice new ones.

Crowbar This helps you to lever out nails and to lift boards and panels.

Stanley knife Keep this old favourite on hand if you need to do some light cutting or trimming.

Slate ripper A specialized tool for cutting and ripping out old roofing nails when replacing roof tiles.

Use a bench plane to keep wood smooth and trim.

Try square

Used as a guide when marking out cladding boards or other materials. Ensures your cut will be perfectly straight and corners truly square.

Plumb line

Handy when you need to mark a true vertical.

Bench plane

This is ideal for trimming end grain and bevelling edges.

What types of tool for patios and paths?

BRICKS AND MORTAR

LAY, LADY, LAY

Bricklaying takes years of practice to perfect. I don't suggest that you attempt a huge building project, but with patience you can certainly manage to rebuild a low garden wall, create a raised flowerbed and even tackle a small repointing job. Patios and paths are also manageable projects. Here are some of the tools that you may need, should you have an urge in the bricks-and-mortar department.

Pointing trowel

A pointed hand tool for shaping the mortar joints between courses of bricks.

Rubber mallet

My favourite! When you're laying your patio, you'll need to gently whack the slabs with this to make sure they are nice and level.

TOOLS TO HIRE

Concrete mixer You can hire one of these for mixing concrete in large quantities. You can either get a great big one or a little cute one, so that you can mix smaller 'large' quantities – if you see what I mean.

Plate vibrator This is an electrically powered flattening machine. Use it when you've laid your patio or path to make sure that all the bricks or slabs are firmly bedded.

Hydraulic guillotine This is a hydraulic device for cutting pavers. It is an absolute 'must' if you have to cut a lot of slabs into awkward shapes.

Club hammer

Use one of these with a brick bolster to cut a brick or stone in half or to size.

Carpenter's pencil

This flat pencil is the only thing to use when marking out bricks or stones – an ordinary pencil point would simply snap in half.

Measuring tape

Keep your steel tape measure handy for all your measuring needs.

Cold chisel

Use this with a hammer for cutting paving slabs, metal and so on.

Brick bolster

Brick bolsters are available in different sizes; the wide blade is perfect for cutting bricks, blocks and paving slabs.

Bricklayer's line and pegs

A nylon line strung between two pegs. Use to mark a straight line for setting out the courses of pavers, bricks, etc.

Gloves

Heavy-duty gloves are a must! Not especially attractive, but if it's them or your fingernails, then I'd choose the gloves every time.

CAN'T DO WITHOUT

Sledgehammer A big, heavy brute, useful for breaking up old paving and masonry, and for general heavy bashing.

Raking tool/plugging chisel Use one of these to remove all the old loose mortar joints when you have a repointing job to do. Place the point in the mortar, then tap the head with a club hammer (*see also page 14*).

Brick trowel This is a fatter sibling of the pointing trowel, used to scoop up and position mortar when laying bricks.

Jointer This is a hand tool with a narrow, rounded blade, used for smoothing out and shaping the mortar joints between brickwork courses, or when pointing.

Try square For accurate marking out.

Crowbar For general prising and levering.

Stiff broom For sweeping up all the mess you've made and for brushing a dry-mix mortar into the joints of paving materials.

Frenchman This is a little hand tool used for scooping up excess mortar from joints. You can make one by heating the end of an ordinary knife, then bending it at right angles (*see page 71*).

Goggles and mask Wear these when handling or cutting abrasive materials.

Spirit level

An absolutely essential tool. If you're laying bricks or paving, you really need to make sure that everything is completely level – both horizontally and vertically.

Getting high

ALL ABOUT LADDERS AND ACCESS EQUIPMENT

Get on up there! Sooner or later you will need a ladder of some sort. A lightweight, aluminium, five- or seven-rung, folding stepladder is sufficient for indoor use. However, the great outdoors is another matter — unless, of course, you live in a very short house. Providing adequate access to the work area is very important indeed, and it really isn't worth compromising your safety by not getting the proper equipment. Teetering and tottering on a makeshift arrangement will only end in tears.

HIRE OPTIONS

☞ Ask the hire company staff to show you how to use this equipment safely.

Scaffold tower Here, sectional frames are joined together to make an access tower. You can build it to the height you need.

Trestles and staging You can hire these to construct a safe and stable work platform to suit your needs.

Work platform This is a little platform unit with a lockable wheel on each leg. Put it where you want it, secure it and up you go.

Dual-purpose ladder
This very clever device converts from a stepladder to a straight ladder. A handy compromise between an ordinary stepladder and an extending ladder.

✱ WHAT'S WITH THE FLYING GOGGLES? WE LIVE IN A BUNGALOW!

ONE DAY, SON, YOU'LL BE AS TALL AS I AM.

LADDER LESSONS

Erecting a ladder Lay the ladder on the ground with the feet against the wall. Raise it slowly to a vertical position while walking towards the wall. Gradually pull the feet away from the wall to a suitable position.

Using a ladder stay It may be the stuff of slapstick movies, but you don't want the feet of the ladder to slip and for you and it to take a dive, so always secure them to the ground using a ladder stay. On soft or uneven ground, place the feet on a piece of board with a batten screwed along one edge. This will prevent the feet of the ladder from sinking or slipping away. Then drive two pegs into the ground next to the batten edge to secure it. Next, tie a piece of rope around the feet and secure it to another peg set firmly into the ground between the feet and the wall. You can buy stabilizers like little metal legs that bolt on to the ladder if the ground is too hard to drive pegs into.

Accessories

Get yourself some accessories to make life aloft more comfortable. A tool tray is a good idea; it clips on to the top of the ladder and holds your tools within easy reach. A paint-kettle hook to hang your paint kettle from is also useful – with one of these you'll always have one hand free with which to hang on to the ladder.

Extending ladder

Double or triple extending ladders are used to get really high. Some are operated by a rope-and-pulley system, so that you can easily extend them yourself.

SO IT'S ONE SMALL STEP FOR A WOMAN, ONE GIANT STEP FOR WOMANKIND!

TIP
Never leave ladders unattended outside your home. Always lock them up securely or store them in a garage or shed, if you have one. An untrustworthy character may take advantage of such an opportunity to break into your home and make off with your valuables.

SAFETY

☞ Do **NOT** be tempted to save a journey up and down by stretching sideways to reach the next bit of work. A stretch too far and you're off the ladder plummeting earthwards.

☞ Never climb higher than four rungs from the top – you'll lose your balance and fall.

☞ Position the foot of a ladder about 1 m (3 ft) out from the wall for every 4 m (12 ft) of the ladder's extended length. A ladder should be leaned at a safe angle – usually around 70 degrees.

☞ When using an extending ladder, make sure the extended sections overlap by at least one quarter of their length.

☞ Always check a ladder before using it. Make sure there is no rotten wood and that the fittings and hinges are in good repair.

Rope
An essential accessory for a ladder stay (*see box above left*).

Here come the big boys

SERIOUS TOOLS FOR HIRE

YEAH, BABE

OK, I know that I'm always stressing the importance of building up a wonderful tool kit, but some things you really do not need to buy. It may be tempting, but resist! Look in the phone book and get the number of your local hire shop — they will have everything you could possibly need for hire at daily rates or, even better, weekend rates. The staff are usually very helpful and will tell you all you need to know about how these gadgets work. They will supply all the accessories and safety equipment, too.

AND HERE'S MORE...

Hydraulic guillotine This is the only machine to use if you have lots of stones or pavers to cut – a real time and effort saver.

Access equipment If you need a really long ladder or an access platform, trestles or a tower, hire one to suit your needs.

Earth rammer Basically a heavy, flat plate on a stick, used for flattening/tamping down earth. Simply hold the handle firmly with both hands, then bash the plate on to the ground.

Angle grinder An electrically powered tool with a heavy-duty revolving blade, used for cutting and shaping brick, stone and metal.

Drain auger

This set comprises a long, flexible coiled wire with a crank-handle at one end. You can hire rods with a variety of attachments for clearing blockages.

Fence-post auger

A tool for making holes for fence posts. If you have a lot of fence posts to set, this will be very useful indeed.

OK, SO I FEEL REALLY SILLY... CAN I COME OUT NOW...PLEASE?

Chainsaw

Use one of these to cut up large logs, or even to cut down an unwanted tree (*see safety box on page 22*).

20

Water pump

If you are unfortunate enough to have a flood in your basement, then you will need one of these to tackle the problem. You can also hire huge hot-air blowers for drying out damp areas.

Concrete mixer

When you have to mix large quantities of concrete, you need to use one of these. They are available in various sizes, and the shop staff will advise you on the correct size for the job.

THE ONLY VIBRATOR THAT YOU CAN PLUG INTO THE MAINS!

Plate vibrator

Once you've laid your patio, use this vibrating machine to ensure that all your slabs or bricks are level and properly bedded.

Circular saw

This is well worth considering if you intend to cut a lot of heavy wood or large sheet materials.

More heavyweights

TOOLS TO TRY THEN BUY

SCARY BUT GOOD!

Say you've hired a piece of heavy-duty equipment just to give it a try, but then find you can't live without it. Go ahead and make that purchase. Some pieces of equipment, such as the pressure washer, are so much fun that you will never want to use elbow grease again!

Hard hat and ear protectors

Wear these to protect yourself from something falling on your head, or when using noisy equipment.

JUST THE THING FOR REALLY BAD HAIR DAYS!

Strimmer

This is handy for trimming straggly bits of grass along the edges or around trees. But don't think you can do a whole lawn with this – it's solely for trimming.

Power saw

This fantastic machine takes the sweat out of sawing. It's hard work being up a ladder, trying to saw off branches. Use the power saw! It can cut pipes, wood and all sorts of other things, too.

SAFETY

☞ Your own personal safety and that of others is of the utmost importance when using power tools outdoors. Always wear the protective clothing provided by the hire shop. Also, warn neighbours if you're using noisy equipment – if you're wearing ear protectors you may not notice a child, pet or person passing by. Better safe than sorry. Test circuit breakers before using an outdoor extension lead with electrical tools and equipment.

Hedge trimmer

If you have an untidy hedge or bush, trim it into a neat shape in no time with this.

Goggles and gloves

Handling scary equipment with sharp blades calls for more heavy-duty goggles and gloves.

SEE HERE, MISTER, I'M GONNA CLEAN UP THIS TOWN WHETHER YOU LIKE IT OR NOT!

ACCESSORIES

Specialized blades and bits

You probably already have a basic set of accessories for your power tools, but if you need a really large masonry bit, a diamond blade for cutting masonry with the circular saw or a long jigsaw blade, then the tool-hire shop will again come to your aid. Just ask them for what you need, and they will undoubtedly come up with the goods – for a small fee, of course. Never attempt to perform a heavy-duty task with an ordinary bit or blade.

Pressure washer

What was I saying about not needing to buy everything? These are so good that you may want one of your own. Use it to clean the car, patio, windows, walls, fences...

Garden shredder

This nifty little garden item is very popular for shredding twigs, leaves and other organic debris.

Tools that come in handy for all kinds of outdoor tasks

ODDBALL TOOLS FOR SPECIFIC JOBS

I love oddball tools and have quite a few tucked away in my toolbox as we speak, just waiting for that special task to present itself! 'Be prepared' — that's my motto. Have a look at this selection — perhaps something will appeal to you. Remember: it pays to get the right tool for the job.

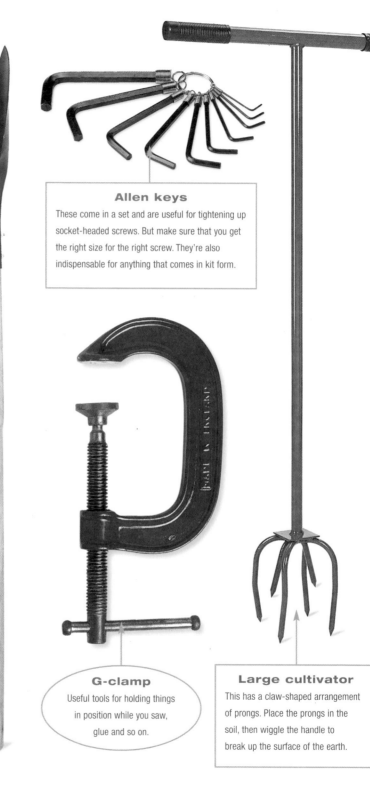

Allen keys

These come in a set and are useful for tightening up socket-headed screws. But make sure that you get the right size for the right screw. They're also indispensable for anything that comes in kit form.

Pipe cutter

A handy gadget that is available in various sizes and specially designed for cutting metal pipes of different diameters.

Fence-post digger

If you intend to do lots of fencing, and need to dig lots of holes, then one of these will probably be a very good purchase. And you can use it for digging holes in general, holes for plants and so on.

G-clamp

Useful tools for holding things in position while you saw, glue and so on.

Large cultivator

This has a claw-shaped arrangement of prongs. Place the prongs in the soil, then wiggle the handle to break up the surface of the earth.

Lopper

Like giant secateurs with long handles, it's very useful when tackling unruly trees and undergrowth. It lops off those branches with ease.

ODDS AND ENDS

Blowtorch Use this for removing very thick paint and for heating up metal pipes for bending.

Mitre saw I think this is a very useful item to own. I have to admit I don't use it that often, but when I do, I think, 'What a fab tool this is!' It enables you to make angled cuts in wood, especially mouldings, and is essential for making picture frames.

Small cultivator

This is the baby to the daddy on the left. Suitable for use in small areas; just place the prongs in the soil, then wiggle it clockwise and anti-clockwise to break up the earth.

Pickaxe

I suspect you will get similar pleasure from wielding a pickaxe, though this tool is more for breaking things up than for demolition – for example, breaking up an old concrete path or paving stones. You can then use the pointed head like a lever to lift and remove the broken pieces.

Sledgehammer

A sledgehammer doesn't fool around. Whenever you need to demolish something, such as a stud partition wall, this is the only way to do it. Wield it with caution, though, as you don't want to demolish more than you bargained for. After a few hefty thwacks you will be a sledgehammer convert.

❋ YOU'VE SIMPLY GOT TO HAVE THE RIGHT TOOLS FOR THE JOB!

Making the earth move

LANDSCAPING TOOLS DIG IT

Are you happy with your landscape? If not, then you may well like to change it — perhaps making it flat where there are bumps or introducing some contours where there is flatness. And if your great outdoors resembles a jungle, then you need some serious defoliation gear. That's the problem with living things such as trees, grass and plants — left to their own devices they just GROW! You have to show them who's boss before it's too late.

Secateurs

A heavy-duty hand snipper for pruning branches and general trimming. Don't try to cut branches or twigs with ordinary household scissors – it will ruin them.

YOU DON'T REALLY NEED A MAN TO CUT THE LAWN, DO YOU?

Pruning/ folding saw

This takes the hard work out of cutting thick twigs or branches – then just folds away afterwards.

I LIKE TO THINK I'M ON THE CUTTING EDGE!

Shears

Like a giant pair of scissors with big handles for general trimming and for tidying undergrowth, such as hedges or bushes. Don't cut thick twigs or branches with these – use a pruning saw.

Mower

There are numerous types, from basic models like this and ones with grass boxes and scarifiers to mini tractor versions. You can tame most lawns with a small-to-average-sized mower.

Fork

Use a fork for breaking up or aerating soil. Place the tines on the earth, then drive them in with the sole of your boot. Wiggle it to break up the earth, then move on to the next spot.

Rake

Use a rake to level out topsoil or fine aggregates.

Hand trowel and rake

It's good to have a few smaller hand tools for minor excavation work, planting and taking care of window boxes.

Hand rake

Hand trowel

MORE ESSENTIALS

Edging tool This has a semi-circular metal blade, perfect for cutting turf into a nice straight line or a gentle curve at the edge of a lawn or flowerbed.

Leaf rake This has a fan arrangement of thin metal prongs to enable you to sweep up all those autumn leaves, ready for the compost bin.

Landscaping material This synthetic fabric has the ability to allow moisture to permeate to the soil underneath, but does not allow weeds to grow through it. Use it when creating patios, paths and other features.

Levelling board A long piece of board, used to tamp down the soil when levelling the ground in preparation for laying a patio or paved area.

Shovel Use for general dirt digging, hole making and earth moving. Make sure you buy one that's easy to handle – that is, not too big – for it'll be heavier once it's laden with earth.

Wheelbarrow

This is a very traditional and particularly lovely item, in my opinion. Simple yet functional – that's what I like. Use it for lugging all sorts of stuff around the garden. Simply load it up, and off you wheel.

Time to get the brushes out!

EXTERIOR DECORATING TOOLS AND EQUIPMENT

A brush is a brush is a brush… Not so, my friend, for there are numerous brushes (and rollers) to suit all sorts of painting and decorating jobs. I've concentrated here on exterior decorating. You'll see some masonry brushes (the big ones) and a few for woodwork; the other items just make life easier for you.

* ALL THESE BRUSHES AND I STILL CAN'T DO A THING WITH MY HAIR!

Dust sheets

Spread dust sheets over areas you don't want to paint, such as the doorstep and patio. This saves you the hassle of cleaning up drips and splashes afterwards.

Woodwork paintbrushes

You can buy a kit containing everything you need for painting woodwork: usually comprising a 38-mm or 50-mm (1½-in or 2-in) paintbrush, plus a paintbrush with angled bristles, used for 'cutting in'.

Masking Tape

What would we do without this stuff? Masking tape is the only thing to use when painting door or window frames. Simply apply a strip of tape to the edges of the glass to protect against splashes.

Wire brush

This is for cleaning and preparing surfaces for painting – the stiff bristles remove dirt, rust and paint particles.

Stippling brush

Masonry paintbrushes

These are generally quite large and sturdy, with stiff bristles. If the surface to be painted is textured, you will need to use a stippling action rather than a brushing one.

Synthetic bristles

Natural bristles

Roller

For outdoor work, invest in an extension handle as well – a real back-saver when painting floors and exterior walls. It's sometimes easier to use a roller and extension than to get up on a ladder and use an ordinary roller.

REALLY CAN'T DO WITHOUT

Paint kettle When you're up a ladder, you don't want to have to haul a giant tin of paint up with you. Decant it into a smaller tin or paint kettle, then hang the kettle from the ladder on a strong wire hook.

Gloves It is always advisable to wear gloves when using exterior paints, since they are not likely to be water-based. Best to avoid getting paint on your hands or you'll have to scrub them and use solvents to get it off.

Glass scraper A handy item if you happen to get a paint splash on your window pane. It has a metal blade set in a plastic handle – just scrape off the paint without damaging the glass.

CARRY THIS OLD THING UP A LADDER? I DON'T THINK SO!

29

Now for the rough stuff

RAW MATERIALS — ALL ABOUT BRICKS AND PAVING

This is the hard (and the very heavy!) stuff — all the materials to build that barbecue or lay that path or patio. Take a trip to your local DIY store or garden centre to check out the variety of slabs, bricks and blocks available before you plan your project — the staff will be happy to give advice. And don't forget to wear gloves when you start work!

Dependable, solid and sturdy — just how I like my men to be!

GORGEOUS PAVING SLABS

👉 You can use rectangular, natural-stone paving slabs or man-made alternatives, which are cheaper. Natural stone looks nicer and weathers more beautifully, so perhaps it's worth saving up for a higher-quality product. For ornamental paving slabs and all kinds of non-rectangular slabs, check out the range of shapes and sizes in your DIY store or garden centre.

BRICKS

👉 Bricks come in all sorts of colours, textures, shapes and types, depending on the type of clay used in their manufacture and the finishing processes. Mortar, a very fine mix of sharp sand and cement, is used for sticking the bricks together. You can buy it in pre-packaged bags of dry mix for convenience – just add water. Bricks basically fall into three categories:

Solid bricks Rectangular, solid bricks, with flat sides all round, though some have a depression called a 'frog' on one side. When laid in courses for building, the frog is filled with mortar and acts as a key.

Cored or perforated bricks The same shape as solid bricks, but these bricks have holes right through them. The holes perform the same function as the frog indentation.

Shaped bricks Specially shaped bricks for decorative additions to walls such as corners, arches, wall tops and so on.

BUILDING BLOCKS

Man-made building blocks are made from poured concrete and are manufactured to various specifications and colours. Some have one textured surface and are used for facing, while others have smooth sides all round for use in general construction. There's a wide variety of blocks to choose from — from solid concrete to decorative pierced-screen blocks. They are bigger than bricks, so wall construction is quicker!

Non-load-bearing blocks
These are generally used for building internal or dividing walls. They are relatively light, being made from a lightweight aggregate, and can be easily cut and shaped.

Pierced-screen block
You can build an entire wall using these lovely decorative blocks, or just lay them at intervals for decoration in a solid wall.

Solid structural concrete block
Most often used for the structural core of a building; usually the surface will be faced or rendered on completion. This type of block is dense and quite heavy.

Cored brick

Perforated brick

Perforated brick

Brick with frog

BRICKS FOR EVERY OCCASION!

✳ SORRY MY HANDS ARE A BIT ROUGH, DARLING, BUT I'VE BEEN LAYING THE PATIO...

More raw stuff for fences and pathways

RAW MATERIALS — SAND, GRAVEL AND WOOD

Here's an assortment of other materials that you'll find useful when you're being creative with pathways in the garden or when you're fencing yourself in — a kind of sticks-and-stones section. The aggregates are usually sold in big heavy bags, so be careful when lifting them. Most garden centres will have samples for you to have a look at before making your selection.

Timber

Stronger, thicker and less flexible than softwood, hardwood timber is ideal for outdoors. There's a huge range, so ask at the timber yard which will be best for a particular job.

GET STUCK IN!

FENCE POSTS

A solid fence must be supported by sturdy fence posts. Panel fences require a few square posts anchored to the ground using metal spikes. Chain-link fences work better with specially designed, pre-drilled concrete or metal posts. Reinforced concrete posts can also be mortised to take horizontal rails or have a vertical groove in which to slot a fence panel.

Round timber fence post A basic type of post for a rustic fencing style. Most timber fence posts you'll find are made from treated softwood, unless you specifically ask for hardwood, which will cost you a lot more money.

Metal fencing spike As an alternative to setting a post in concrete, you can place the lower end of a square fence post into the socket of a big metal spike like this. The spike is driven into the ground using a sledgehammer, then the fence post is inserted.

Square fence post These posts are designed to be used in conjunction with metal fencing spikes and are available in various sizes. They can also be set in concrete as a more permanent installation.

Decking timber

Fence board

Round timber fence post

Metal fencing spike

Square fence post

CONCRETE INGREDIENTS

Concrete consists of Portland cement mixed with fine aggregate (sand), coarse aggregate (gravel or crushed stone) and water. When water is added to the dry ingredients, it triggers a chemical reaction in which the cement forms a paste that binds the aggregates into one of the strongest and most versatile of building materials. The ingredients are mixed in different proportions depending on the intended use and desired strength of the concrete. A typical mix consists of 1 part cement, 2½ parts sand and 3 parts gravel or crushed stone.

Sand

☞ Sand for concrete should be coarse and free of silt and debris. Do not use beach sand or fine builder's (mortar) sand.

Cement

☞ This looks like a fine grey powder and is sold dry, in great big bags, from builders' merchants and DIY stores.

Gravel

☞ Varies in size, shape and colour. Some are rounded, others sharper and more jagged. Gravel for concrete should be clean and free of debris.

Aggregate

☞ Fine and coarse aggregates (i.e. sand and gravel or crushed stone) for making concrete are sold by the cubic metre or cubic yard. The package information will help you calculate correct quantities.

Post-setting mix

☞ A pre-packaged sand, cement and aggregate dry mix used for setting fence posts in the ground. Insert the post, pack with the dry mix and add water.

LET ME PUT MY HANDS IN YOUR CEMENT! IT'LL BE JUST LIKE HOLLYWOOD!

All you need for a great exterior

RAW MATERIALS — WET FINISHES

Paints and primers, stains and varnishes — all sorts of wet stuff to prepare, and with which to beautify all your exterior surfaces, from metal to masonry, the deck to the garden shed. You can guarantee there will be a multitude of fabulous products on the market from which to choose. These days loads of new colours and shades are arriving on the shelves all the time. Do not use an indoor product outdoors, because it is not likely to withstand adverse weather conditions and you'll only be disappointed with the result.

Masonry paint

Available in a smooth or textured finish, this is extremely durable, colourfast and waterproof. It is suitable for all exterior masonry and brickwork.

Exterior gloss paint

This is really tough stuff for exterior woodwork, such as doors and window frames. Some exterior paint products can also be used on metal, downpipes and gates. It gives a beautiful glossy, hardwearing, weather-resistant finish. It won't last for ever, but it will certainly look great for many years.

✱ NOW IF I WANT A SLEEK, SOPHISTICATED VIBE, I GO FOR TEAK OIL.

Paint stripper

Paint strippers are highly caustic chemical substances and must be handled with care. Apply, wait and watch the paint bubble, then remove it with a scraper. Wear gloves – this stuff will burn your skin.

TEAK OIL, WOOD STAIN AND PRIMER

After initial preparation, a good result depends on adequate priming. Whether it is wood, metal or masonry, each surface should be primed to provide a good base for the top coat. There are primers suitable both for ferrous (metal that is likely to rust) and non-ferrous surfaces (galvanized items, for instance). Just choose the right one for the job. If you don't want to use paint, then try wood stain or furniture oil.

Wood stain Various products are available. Wood stain adds colour or wood tones to hard- and softwoods, from fences to sheds and decks. It is designed to protect the wood, yet still allow the beauty of the natural grain to show through.

Teak oil/furniture oil Give your poor old, weather-beaten hardwood furniture a new lease of life with some oil. It replaces the natural essential oils that are necessary to prevent the wood from drying out; it restores the original colour, too.

Wood primer All bare wood needs to be primed before beginning the undercoating and painting. The wood primer penetrates the surface of the wood, creates a good base for the top coats, and ensures better top coat coverage.

Floor paint

Heavy-duty garage floor paint

Teak oil

Exterior varnish

Wood stain

35

What you need for lighting and water features

SPARKLE AND SPLASH!

SPECIAL-PURPOSE ITEMS — WORKING WITH LIGHT AND WATER

DIY antics in the garden do not just include decorating, construction work and general undergrowth-taming. You could consider your garden to be kind of an outdoor room, complete with running water and lights — be they decorative or functional. Take a look around your local DIY store or garden centre. You'll find lots of do-it-yourself kits for lighting and water features such as ponds and sprinklers — you name it. The garden is not just a place to hang your washing!

OUTDOOR LIGHTS

Decorative lighting Low-voltage lights and solar garden-lighting products are available in great abundance these days. They can be used with delicate tree lights to create a romantic and subtle atmosphere, or as accents along paths or walkways. Simply choose the ones you like best.

Functional lighting You will find a huge range of security-lighting products at any DIY store, from a simple entrance light to a full-scale floodlight kit. You'll surely find something to suit your needs.

Spade
Useful for shovelling just about anything and for digging holes. It's good to have a matching set of spade and fork.

Edging tool
Use a semi-circular blade to dig out light-cable or water-pipe channels and the pipework channels for sprinkler systems.

Globe light

Security light

Accent light

Note
If you would like a permanent power point outside, get a professional to install it for you.

Water pump

Water pumps can be bought separately or as part of a kit, to create either a water feature or fountain. Water pumps are powered by electricity, which is usually passed through a transformer, reducing the current and making the whole operation safe.

OTHER USEFUL ITEMS

Hand tools For any kind of electrical work, you'll need your screwdriver set and wire cutters or pliers.

Pond liner This is heavy-duty, flexible plastic or rubber sheeting, used to line the great big hole that you're going to dig for the pond to house your koi.

Bucket Its purpose is obvious, but do make sure yours doesn't have a hole in it.

Wellington boots Wear good waterproof boots or shoes when working in a watery situation to keep your feet warm and dry.

Bricklayer's line and pegs/chalk line For marking out the position of electrical lines or sprinkler-pipe channels.

YOU NEVER KNOW, THERE COULD BE A PALACEFUL OF FROGS UNDER THOSE LILY PADS.

✳ KISS ME! GO ON, KISS ME! OH, PLEASE! KISS ME!

WHEN I SAID I FELT LIKE CHINESE, I MEANT WONTONS WITH NOODLES AND A PILE OF PRAWN CRACKERS...

Putting your back into a job without putting pain into your back

LOOKING AFTER YOURSELF IN THE GREAT OUTDOORS

'Lift that barge, tote that bale.' There's a right way and a wrong way to do everything, and believe you me you don't want to be doing it the wrong way when there's heavy stuff to lift.

Back injuries are painful and recurring, so please don't take any risks. If you're going to lift a heavy load, never, never bend at the waist, with your legs straight and knees locked. Attempt to lift the load this way and you will injure your back. See the box below for correct lifting procedures!

HOW TO LIFT HEAVY STUFF

☞ Stand close to the object to be lifted and then slowly bend at the knees, keeping your back straight until you are able to grasp the object. Keeping your back as straight as possible, looking directly in front of you, straighten your knees and lift the load. The object is lifted successfully, without sustaining an injury to your back. Never bend forward with your knees straight!

* THIS BEATS DOING PUSH-UPS AND AB CRUNCHES AT THE GYM!

Back
Keep your back straight and never bend forward.

Hands
Lifting heavy loads can really chafe your hands, so wear protective gloves!

Lifting
When you've loaded the barrow, stand between the handles, bend your knees and grasp the handles. Then straighten your knees to lift the wheelbarrow off its legs.

Crowbar

A couple of crowbars are always handy, taking the strain out of prising awkward or heavy objects off, up or out.

Levers

Here's how a lever works: you have your heavy load, the lever (a plank of wood or a crowbar) and a fulcrum (the point at which the lever pivots). Place the lever on the fulcrum, with one end under the load, while you stand at the other end exerting pressure downwards. The result – the load is lifted. Imagine it like a seesaw: when you press down, the load goes up. You can also use a sort of 'rowing' action in order to shift the load along bit by bit, rather than up.

PRACTICAL FASHION

Clothing For outdoor work in a cold climate, wear thermal underwear to keep you cosy. A body warmer is also good because it allows free and unrestricted movement of the arms. In warm and sunny weather, you can wear a bikini top and shorts, but it's probably best to wear proper trousers to protect your skin from scratches and scrapes – and remember the sunscreen. And if you're going to do a lot of painting, invest in some overalls, to save your clothes.

Footwear Wear sturdy boots, preferably with steel toe caps if you are doing anything with heavy stones or pavers.

Accessories Tool belt – a handy little round-the-waist, bits-and-pieces carrier.

Headgear The old favourites: goggles and mask. They are made for comfort and safety – definitely not for style. If in doubt, wear both: it's better to look a fright than have grit in the eye and a lungful of dust. Wear a hard hat, too, if there's a danger of falling objects.

Hands Use the safety gloves for anything that'll be harsh on the mitts. For lighter work, use a good protective hand cream. Then, when you've finished for the day, wash your hands with a heavy-duty hand cleanser to remove any ground-in grime. Next, put on some fragrant hand cream. To prevent dirt from getting stuck inside your nails, scratch a bar of soap before going outside to work. Just wash away later.

Tool bag An invaluable tool-carrier.

I ALWAYS RELAX IN THE LOTUS POSITION AFTER A HARD DAY LIFTING TOADSTOOLS.

39

SHEDDING THE LOAD

A place for everything and everything in its place. Good organization really is the key to storage success in the great outdoors.

Storage solutions

STORAGE IN the garden can be a headache sometimes, can't it? Just what do you do with all those tins of paint, garden tools, paintbrushes, watering cans, buckets — need I go on? I'm sure you don't need stuff cluttering up your home, especially if indoor space is at a premium. Find your answer in these simple storage solutions for your garage, shed or basement. They are very easy to achieve, and the best thing is that they will cost you next to nothing!

USING YOUR SHED EFFECTIVELY

Do you have a neglected shed in your garden? Does it have good storage potential but needs some general maintenance and a bit of cosmetic attention? First, check that the shed is structurally sound — if it really is falling down or unsafe, then demolish it and build a new one on the same base (*see pages 44–47*). However, if it's simply a bit old and tired, then give it a new lease of life. Just grab your tool kit and some paintbrushes.

* BUT WHERE AM I GOING TO PUT THE SAUNA?

* HMM... NOW WHAT TO DO WITH THOSE DUSTY OLD BOOKS?

Hell's Angel

Never buy stuff that won't fit through the shed door!

QUICK STORAGE MAKEOVER

Preliminary check-up: make sure the shed panels are firmly attached to each other at the corners. If the joints are loose, simply retighten the screws. Oil the door hinges and replace them if they are rusty. Finally, have a look at the roofing felt: is it secure? Does it leak? If it is loose, reattach it with galvanized nails. If it needs to be replaced, that's easy: just remove the old stuff, buy some new stuff and attach it with more galvanized nails. Now let's move on to some simple storage solutions.

A GIRL NEEDS ALL THE SUPPORT SHE CAN GET!

1. Simple metal shelf brackets like these are very cheap and readily available just about everywhere. All you have to do is mark the position of your shelf or shelves on the studs (vertical supports) of your shed. Use a spirit level to make sure that the brackets are all at the same height.

2. Now screw the shelf brackets securely in place. Place commercial shelving or a simple plank of wood cut to size on the shelf brackets, then screw the brackets to the underside of the shelf just to make sure it will stay put when loaded. You will need one bracket at each end of a short shelf, and one or more in the middle if it's long.

3. Once the shelf is finished, simply wash and remove the labels from all your empty screw-top glass jars, then attach the lids (two screws each) to the underside of your lowest shelf. Fill the jars with screws, nails and so on, then screw them into the lids. This makes good use of space under shelves, and because you can see through the glass, there's no need for labels. Easy!

TWINE DISPENSERS

☞ Another use for those empty jam jars. Wash and remove the labels, then make a hole through the centre of the lids with a hammer and centre punch. Place a ball of string or twine in each jar, pass the end through the hole in the lid and screw the lid back on to the jar. You can now pull the string/twine from the jar when you need it without it getting tangled up.

BOOKCASE ORGANIZER

☞ Never throw away an old bookcase! You may not need it in your home any more, but there will always be a place for it in the shed, garage or basement. It's a good idea to store your paint tins and solvents away from your living area for safety anyway, so a little shelf unit is just perfect. Load the other shelves with all the other bits and pieces that you don't have space for indoors. You could also screw some small cup hooks or tool-clips to the sides of the bookcase to hold small hand tools or other items.

Construct your own fabulous storage space

BUILDING A SHED FROM A KIT

What? No shed? But it's easy to build one yourself! Most big DIY stores and garden centres sell inexpensive sheds in all shapes and sizes. Just measure the space you have available in your garden, then decide which shed would fit it best. It will arrive in giant kit form, and will usually consist of a floor deck, four sides, a roof, a roll of roofing felt, a window, a set of instructions (don't lose these) and a bag of nails, pins and screws. The first thing you need to do is read the instructions very carefully and familiarize yourself with all the bits and pieces. Check that everything is present and correct, then begin the assembly. The instructions will tell you exactly which screws and nails to use for each step.

TIP

When laying the paved base, try to use complete paving slabs so that you won't have to cut them.

1 Prepare the area. This is very important: you can't just build a shed on the bare earth and hope for the best. It needs a dry and solid base to sit on. (*Refer to pages 116–17 for levelling ground and page 118 for laying a paved patio.*) Basically, a shed base consists of level, compacted ground with a sheet of landscaping material to fend off any weed growth, a layer of sand and paving slabs on top.

2 The floor of the shed will already have been constructed and prepared for you, so all you have to do is position it squarely on the paving slabs.

3 Place the gabled back and one side panel in position on the shed floor. Drill clearance holes and then screw the lower edges of the side frames to the base, using the large screws provided. Then nail the two panels together at the corner.

4 Install and secure the remaining side panel and the gabled front to the floor in the same way. Screw through to the floor and then nail the panels together at the corner. At each stage check that the corners are at right angles and that the walls are vertical – use a try square and a spirit level.

TIP

Wear gloves when handling shed panels or you may end up with a splinter.

5 Place the first roof section in position (it doesn't matter which side you do first). Make sure that the top edge is exactly lined up with the apex of the front and back panels. Nail it securely to the shed frame.

6 Next comes the second roof section. This fits on to the shed in exactly the same way as the first. Make sure that the top edge butts neatly against the top edge of the first section at the apex – you don't want any gaps.

7 Using the Stanley knife, cut two lengths of roofing felt about 10 cm (4 in) longer than the roof, measuring from front to back. Place one length on the roof, overlapping the apex and protruding beyond the other three edges by about 5 cm (2 in). Nail roofing felt to the frame along the eaves. Space the nails at intervals of about 20 cm (8 in).

need

* gloves
* paving slabs
* landscaping material
* sand
* spirit level
* try square
* sledgehammer
* levelling board
* hammer
* galvanized nails
* screwdriver
* drill
* Stanley knife

8 Apply the second length of roofing felt in the same way, nailing along the eaves as before. Then nail the overlap securely to the roof near the apex. Roofing felt is gritty, messy stuff to deal with, so make sure that you brush your clothes off afterwards.

✳ IF SHE CAN BUILD A SHED, I SURE CAN, TOO!

45

9 Nail a corner strip to each of the four corners of the shed. These thin wooden battens finish the construction off nicely and seal the corners against the weather.

10 Fold the edges of the roofing felt neatly at each of the four corners and at the front and back of the apex. You can trim the felt a little at this stage if you've made the overlap too big.

11 Attach the barge boards, which are simply boards with mitred ends. Nail two boards along the edge of the roof at the front and the back, making sure the mitred ends meet neatly at the apex. The boards hold the edges of the roofing felt securely. To add a touch of individuality, you can use wider boards and cut the edges and ends of the boards into a decorative shape.

12 Those two diamond-shaped pieces of wood are called 'finials', and are used at the apex of the shed roof at the front and the back. Just hammer them into place using two nails. The purpose of the finials is twofold. They add a decorative finishing touch and they also cover the joint between the barge boards.

※ SHE SURE HAS A WAY WITH WOOD!

13 The shed kit will not include real glass for the windows; instead, there will be a pre-cut piece of clear perspex – this is much safer! Place the perspex into the window frame. It should not need to be trimmed.

14 You will have three thin wooden battens left over. These are the glazing strips that will hold the glazing material firmly in the window frame. Place a strip along each side and across the lower edge of the frame, then nail them securely in place.

15 Last but not least, attach the little metal turn-button about halfway up the door frame, using the screw provided. This ensures that the shed door will stay firmly shut.

❋ AT LAST, A HOME OF MY OWN!

TOO GOOD JUST TO KEEP TOOLS IN!

AND PLANNING

☞ This is a basic tool shed, which you can build yourself. However, you can buy more sophisticated versions. If you want to attempt a larger, more ambitious project, then be sure to check with your local authority first. There may be restrictions regarding size and positioning, particularly in rural areas, so you may need the authority's approval before you proceed. You don't want to build a masterpiece and then have to make it smaller or demolish it!

Cosmetic surgery for sheds MORE MORE MORE

PAINTING A SHED 2

All exterior wood needs to be protected from the elements with stain, paint or a wood sealant. Exterior-quality wood finishes are available in many fabulous colours. I chose wood stains in subtle blues and sage green. The wax-enriched formula is quick-drying, water-repellent and not harmful to plants or pets. It can be used on fences and rough-sawn exterior woodwork, too. Load a paintbrush well and apply the stain in thick, even coats. Do not spread the stain out too much, as this can result in a patchy finish. Paint all the stripes in one colour first, then proceed with the next colour. One coat should be enough, but if it needs another when the stain is dry, simply recoat in the same way.

FITTING A NEW LOCK 3

👉 If you are using your shed to store tools or other valuable items, you will need to consider security. A simple hasp and staple, along with a sturdy padlock, should be enough to keep the shed secure and act as a deterrent to casual intruders.

need

- hasp and staple with screws
- padlock
- bradawl
- screwdriver

1 Mark the position of the hasp on the door, then mark the position of the staple in a corresponding position on the door frame. Make pilot holes for the screws in the wood with a bradawl. It is vital for the parts to line up exactly or you will have difficulty closing the hasp over the staple.

2 Screw both parts securely into position. Close the hasp on to the staple, then pass the padlock through it. A locking device like this is quite secure, because when closed, the screw heads are completely covered, thus making them more difficult to remove.

MAKING A WINDOW BOX

OK, maybe this is a bit extravagant, but it is a cute finishing touch. Fill window boxes with real or fake flowers, depending on whether you like high- or low-maintenance gardening!

1 For the window box, simply cut three pieces of timber a little longer than the width of the window, and cut two more pieces to about 10 cm (4 in) in length. Screw the two short-end pieces to two of the long pieces to form the sides (drill clearance holes first). Then screw the last piece to the base to complete the box.

2 Attach the two brass plate hangers to the top edge of the back of the window box. You can then attach the box easily to the shed with two screws.

need
* scraps of 150-mm x 25-mm (6-in x 1-in) timber
* drill
* screws
* brass plate hangers
* screwdriver

❋ DO YOU THINK GEORGE WILL RUN UP SOME CURTAINS FOR ME IF I ASK NICELY?

ADDING CURTAINS

☞ Curtains are a nice finishing touch to your shed. Cut two pieces of fabric as wide as the window and about 30 cm (12 in) longer than the height. Stitch a narrow double hem down both sides of both pieces, then fold and stitch a 2-cm (¾-in) double hem across the top and bottom edges. Cut a piece of curtain wire a little shorter than the width of the window and screw an eye to each end. Pass the wire though the top hem of each curtain. Screw the hook to each side of the top of the window frame, then hang up the curtains. If you like, you could also make some tie-backs from strips of fabric or ribbons.

need
* pretty curtain fabric
* curtain wire
* two screwhooks and eyes
* scissors, pins, thread, etc.

A girl just can't have too many shelves

PUTTING UP ADJUSTABLE SHELVES

Adjustable shelving is a perfect way to make the best use of wall space in your shed, garage or basement because you can adjust the size to suit your storage needs. A wide range of adjustable shelving systems is available from DIY stores. All you have to do is secure the shelving uprights in position and then add the shelving brackets where desired!

1 Consider your wall area and decide where you'd like the shelves to be. If you are attaching the shelves to a stud wall, bear in mind that the uprights should be screwed into studs. One major consideration is height: you need to be able to reach them easily. Mark the position of each upright with a faint pencil line and use a spirit level to make sure that it's vertical. Then mark the top of each upright – again, use the spirit level to make sure the marks are horizontal.

2 Place one upright in position. Mark the position of the topmost screw. Drill a hole at the mark and insert a wall plug. Loosely drive a screw through the upright's top hole into the plug. Make sure the upright is vertical and then mark the other screw-hole positions. Do this with all the uprights in turn.

3 Gently swing the upright out of the way, then drill a hole at each marked position. Insert a wall plug into each hole.

4 Screw all the uprights securely to the wall. Remember to tighten the topmost screw. You can now insert all the shelving brackets. Each has a shaped end that hooks into the uprights and supports the shelves at the height required.

need
- drill
- wall plugs
- screws
- screwdriver
- spirit level
- pencil
- shelving uprights
- shelving brackets
- shelves

PUTTING UP A PEGBOARD WALL PANEL

Perforated hardboard, or 'pegboard', has small pre-drilled holes all over it. Buy wire hooks in all shapes and sizes, then organize them as you please on the pegboard to hold tools and equipment.

need

drill	spirit level
wall plugs	pencil
screws	sheet pegboard
screwdriver	screw cups

1 Hold the panel up to the wall, then mark the corner position of the pegboard panel on the wall with faint pencil lines.

2 Mark, drill and plug screw holes at each corner and at 20-cm (8-in) intervals along each side. Ensure that the marks correspond with the predrilled holes in the board along the sides. Now slip a screw cup on to each screw before securing the panel to the wall.

PUTTING UP BIKE/LADDER HOOKS

☞ Large heavy-duty hooks are the only way to hang up heavy items like ladders or bicycles. They come in various sizes to suit all needs. Simply secure the hooks in a suitable position, then hang up your stuff.

need

- drill
- wall plugs
- screws
- screwdriver
- spirit level
- pencil
- heavy-duty ladder/bike hooks

1 Mark the position of each hook using a spirit level. Each hook must be at the same height as its partner so that your bike or ladder will hang straight. If the hooks are widely spaced, use a long wooden batten to span the area between the marks, then place the level on top.

2 Hold the hook up to the wall and mark each screw hole with a pencil dot. Drill the holes, drive in plugs, then screw the hook into place. Secure the other hook/hooks in position to complete your hanging system.

TIP
For drilling screw holes in masonry, use a masonry bit and insert a wall plug into the hole. If you insert screws directly into the wall, they will come loose in no time.

More storage

ADDING TOOL HOOKS TO PEGBOARD

8

Your outdoor tools may be large and cumbersome, and even a bit grubby, so you wouldn't really want to drag them inside your house and ruin your interior home improvement! Adding tool hooks is the perfect way to organize outdoor tools in your shed, garage or basement.

1 Insert the tool hooks into the pegboard panel. Each hook will have two prongs especially for this purpose. You may have to squeeze the prongs together a little to fit them into the holes.

2 Place the hooks in a row at intervals of about 5 cm (2 in) to accommodate garden tool handles. Hooks like these are available in all shapes and sizes; simply choose those that suit your needs.

need

long pegboard tool hooks

WHEELBARROW STORAGE

9

👉 What do you do with a wheelbarrow when it's not in use? Park it in the garden upside-down and you're likely to trip over it. Why not hang it up? Use offcuts of scrap wood to make this simple hanging device.

1 Using a tenon saw, cut 35-cm (14-in) lengths of 25-mm x 25-mm (1-in x 1-in) and 50-mm x 25-mm (2-in x 1-in) timber (one each). Glue and screw them together to form an L-shape to hold the base of the barrow. Now cut a piece of 50-mm x 25-mm (2-in x 1-in) timber to fit between the handles of the barrow.

2 Cut two shorter pieces to act as turn-buttons to hold the handles. Screw the turn-buttons to the larger piece, as shown.

3 Mark the position of both parts of the wheelbarrow holder on the wall. Drill and plug, then screw the pieces into place. Hang up the wheelbarrow by placing the edge of the pan in the lower L-shape, then rest the handles on the wall (on either side of the upper holder). Swivel the turn-buttons to hold the handles.

need

* drill and wall plugs
* screwdriver and screws
* spirit level and pencil
* offcuts of 50-mm x 25-mm (2-in x 1-in) timber
* scraps of 25-mm x 25-mm (1-in x 1-in) timber
* tenon saw and wood glue

MAKING GALVANIZED MESH STORAGE BOXES

10

Galvanized metal mesh is ideal for use indoors and outdoors because it is rustproof. Also, if you use these boxes to store stuff outside, they don't fill with water.

need
* one sheet of galvanized 25-mm (1-in) wire mesh, about 90 cm x 60 cm (3 ft x 2 ft)
* side cutters

1 Place the mesh sheet on a flat surface, then work from one short side inwards. Using the side cutters, snip a slot that is one square wide and nine squares long, about five squares in from the edge.

2 Fold up the two long side sections of the mesh sheet at right angles to the base, then fold in the end pieces at right angles to the sides. This forms the basic rectangular shape of the box.

3 Fold the projecting ends around the short sides, then tuck them inside. Your wonderful new storage box will now hold its shape quite securely without extra fastenings.

TIP

Avoid using cardboard boxes, especially for storage in the shed or a damp environment. Cardboard will absorb moisture and become soft – a problem when you lift it up and the bottom falls out!

* YES! YES! YES! RUST-FREE STORAGE AT LAST!

AND YOU THOUGHT BASKETWORK WAS JUST FOR THERAPY!

MORE STORAGE IDEAS

☞ Keep your eyes peeled for other boxes that may be cheap or free! Your local greengrocer may throw away light, plywood orange boxes regularly. Simply rescue them from the rubbish and then paint with the colour of your choice. Great for storing bits and pieces.

££

Junk potting table

11

THIS OLD sideboard was an irresistible car-boot-sale find. I just fell in love with its cool retro shape and thought it would look perfect in the garden as a potting table and storage cabinet in one. This kind of transformation is frighteningly easy, girls. All you have to do is add a coat of colourful exterior paint to protect the wood from the elements, then make a shiny, new aluminium cover for the top. To complete, just screw a few large hooks in each side to hang your hand tools or gloves on. You can chalk 'outdoor repairs to do' lists on the blackboard doors or draw little pictures to remind you of what's been stored inside.

FROM JUNK
TO JEWEL
IN NO TIME!

1 Remove the doors and drawers, then sand all surfaces thoroughly to remove old varnish and to create a good base for paint. Use an electric sander to make your job easier (sanding is hard work).

need

* junk cabinet or sideboard
* sander and dust mask
* white spirit
* soft cloth
* primer
* exterior paint
* blackboard paint
* paintbrush and gloves
* piece of thin aluminium
* Stanley knife
* metal rule
* tin snips
* wooden batten
* centre punch
* bradawl
* hammer
* four domed chrome screws
* four chrome screw cups
* screwdriver
* screw hooks

2 Remember that sanding is a very dusty activity, so wear a protective mask. When you've finished the job, wipe all the surfaces clean with a cloth or rag soaked in white spirit.

3 Apply a coat of primer to the bare wood on the sideboard carcass and the door and drawer fronts. When the primer is dry, paint the carcass and the small cabinet doors with green exterior paint and the large doors and drawer fronts with blackboard paint. Allow all the paint to dry, then apply a second coat if necessary.

4 Ask your local metal supplier to cut a piece of thin aluminium for you that overlaps the top of the old cabinet or sideboard by approximately 2.5 cm (1 in) all round. Measure, mark and score a line 2.5 cm (1 in) in from each side of the metal rectangle. Use a Stanley knife and a metal rule to do this.

5 Snip into the corner as shown, then bend the metal along the score lines using a batten as a guide. It's a good idea to wear gloves while you do this to keep you from cutting your fingers. Bend all four sides to shape in this way, making sure that the corners are folded in neatly.

HOW NICE IS THIS? GO ON, MAKE YOUR OWN!

6 Place the metal worktop in position on the sideboard. Punch holes through the metal at each corner, using the hammer and centre punch. Then pierce a pilot hole for the screw in the wood underneath using a bradawl.

7 Slip a screw cup onto each of the chrome screws, then secure the top in place by screwing through the holes into the sideboard frame. Finally, remove the protective plastic film from the metal worktop and screw a few large hooks to each side to dangle your hand tools from. Use coloured chalk to draw a few pretty pictures on the doors just for fun!

KEEPING UP APPEARANCES

Basic fixes for exteriors, from roofs and drains to walls and windows, plus lots of little extras that you might find useful in the great outdoors.

Top-to-toe exterior maintenance

Prevention is, as always, better than cure. Solve small problems before they become big ones: locate loose tiles, find problematic downpipes and clear minor blockages in drains before they turn into major ones. Regular maintenance can save you money in the long run. This section shows you that simple exterior maintenance isn't as scary as it looks — you'll be replacing downpipes, renovating cladding, attaching storm windows, fitting an outdoor tap and much, much more — and still have time to paint your nails afterwards.

HELLO, ROOF!

It's worth investing in a pair of binoculars. Why? Well, every now and then (twice a year should suffice), they will enable you to take a close look at the condition of your roof from the safety of terra firma. Spot small problems before they get out of hand: loose tiles, wobbly downpipes and so on. Make inspections after storms or bad weather, because strong winds tend to lift tiles or slates, which in turn allows water to penetrate the roof cavity.

✳ DON'T GO LOOKING WHERE YOU SHOULDN'T BE LOOKING!

ROOFING MATERIALS AND FORMS

Unless you need to replace the whole roof, you'll have to live with what you've got and replace the odd tile or slate now and then. Most roof coverings are either cut from natural materials such as slate, or moulded from clay or concrete.

Bonnet hip tiles
✳ Curved to fit round the outside edge of a roof hip.

Standard tiles
✳ Cover most of the roof. They are slightly convex and have nail holes along the top edge.

Ridge and hip tiles
✳ Curvy or pointy, they cover the gap where roof slopes meet at the top (ridge) or side (hip).

Valley tiles
✳ Cover where two slopes meet at the bottom.

ANATOMY OF A ROOF

In its most basic form, an ordinary gable roof is triangular in shape, which is a good load-bearing shape. The weight of the roof is carried by sloping rafters that meet at the apex of the roof, the 'ridge'. To keep the roof from pushing out the walls of the house, the bases of the rafters are joined together horizontally by joists. However, many roofs have additional hipped ends, dormer windows or extended parts, making them quite complicated structures. The diagram shows a typical roof with hips, ridges, valleys and various other features. The cross-section shows a simple three-layer construction: rafters first, then roofing felt, then roofing battens to hold the felt secure, and finally roof coverings — tiles, slates and so on. There are a few danger spots to keep a careful eye on: flashings around chimneys or dormer windows, valleys in which one plane of the roof meets another, and ridges or hipped ends on which the tiles might slip or be lifted by the wind. Be vigilant and you won't have too much to worry about.

FLASHINGS

A few words about flashings. These are strips of material – most commonly lead, but sometimes zinc, roofing felt or mortar fillets – used to weatherproof the joints between the roof and other parts. You'll find flashing strips along valleys and abutments between chimneys, dormers and walls, and where one roof meets another. They can wear out or sustain damage over the years, causing leaks. Replacement flashing is readily available from DIY stores in order to make small repairs.

DAMP-PROOF COURSE

CHIMNEY

APRON

FASCIA

GABLE END

BARGE BOARD

FLASHING

ROOFING BATTENS OVER ROOFING FELT

METAL VALLEY

SLATES OR TILES

RIDGE TILE

HIPPED END

HIP TILE

GUTTERS

EAVES

ROOFING FELT

RAFTER

Letting yourself loose up on the roof

REPLACING A LOOSE SLATE

12

A slate may work itself loose due to a break or crack, or perhaps the fixing nails have corroded, allowing it to slip. Replace it immediately — high winds love to work their way under a loose slate and strip it and its neighbours off. Any material has a limited life, so if your roof is old and in bad shape, then small repairs should only be considered as a temporary fix while you save up for a full or partial replacement. If you do decide to make a repair, try to use a slate that matches the existing ones as closely as possible.

SPOTTING LEAKS

Leaks are a common problem for home owners. Sometimes the causes and remedies are clear, but at other times the sources of leaks will be a little elusive and you will have to resort to detective work. Settle in the loft on a rainy day (a torch helps), and wait and watch. Eventually you'll discover where the water is coming in. It might not be obvious: water can be sneaky. When the source has been identified, you can start fixing the leak. Always try to repair a small leak before it gets to be a deluge – it won't go away if you ignore it!

1 Use a slate ripper to cut and remove the nails that hold the slate in place. Slip the tool under the broken slate and hook the end around the nail. Hammer on the slate ripper's knee to try to either remove the nail or cut through it. If the slate has slipped off by itself, you will need to remove old nails anyway before you can insert the new one.

2 Remove the old, damaged slate. It won't be possible for you to nail the new slate into position, so get a lead or zinc strip about 2.5 cm (1 in) longer than the depth of the slate. Nail the top end of the strip to the roofing batten underneath. To do this the nail must pass through the gap between the tiles of the previous course.

3 Position the new slate on top of the lead or zinc strip, then slide it into place. The lower edge of the new slate should match up exactly with the edges of the slates on each side so that it doesn't look out of line. When you are satisfied with the positioning, you can fold the end of the metal strip over the lower edge of the slate to hold it securely.

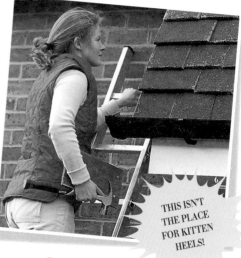

THIS ISN'T THE PLACE FOR KITTEN HEELS!

need
* slate ripper
* hammer
* lead or zinc strip
* nails
* new slate

REPAIRING A BROKEN TILE

A broken or cracked tile may be a bit tricky to remove. The moulded interlocking or overlapping shape of each tile has little retaining 'nibs' on the back. These nibs hold the tiles securely in position, but also make them difficult to remove! Use a few wooden wedges to make the task easier.

need
* new tile
* wooden wedges
* slate ripper

Who would have thought wedges could be so useful?

❶ Locate the offending tile. If it is in an overlapping pattern (as pictured), you will need to raise the tiles on either side. If it is interlocking, then you may also have to raise the one above and to the left.

❷ To remove the tile you will need to ease it up from the roofing batten on which it rests. Drive wooden wedges gently under the surrounding tiles, then try to ease the broken one free. If it's attached with a nail, then you will need to either wiggle it loose or cut it, using a slate ripper to free the tile. Now insert a new tile into the gap and remove the wedges.

❋ THIS IS AS HIGH AS I LIKE TO GET!

REPLACING FELT SHINGLES

Felt shingles are occasionally used for roofing, and they come in a variety of colours. Curled or slightly torn shingles can be repaired by gluing them down with bitumen adhesive and reinforcing them with galvanized roofing nails.

❶ Carefully lift the uppermost good shingle using a crowbar. Remove the first row of nails that are holding down the damaged shingle by slipping the crowbar underneath the damaged shingle and pulling upwards. After removing the nails, gently pull out the broken shingle pieces. Slide the new shingle up into place and align it carefully with the neighbouring shingles.

❷ When the new shingle is in position, carefully secure it in place with four galvanized roofing nails. Use the crowbar to hammer the new nails into position – this allows you to drive in the new nails without damaging or bending the shingles above. Place the crowbar over the top of the nail head and hammer on the crowbar a little way along it and away from the upper shingle.

Keeping it all covered

REPLACING A BUILT-UP FLAT ROOF

15

Flat roofs can sometimes be problematic for the people who live underneath them. Traditional rag-fibre bitumen roofing felt tends to become brittle with age, and leaks can be difficult to detect on flat roofs because the water can run downhill from the entry point before seeping through. A major replacement job for a house should be left to the professionals, but a flat roof on a small shed or garage should be within your reach. The materials you need are readily available from DIY stores and builders' merchants, sometimes in kit form. Keep an eye on the forecasts because you'll need dry, calm weather for this job. Begin by removing the old felt. This is messy and dusty work, so wear protective gloves and a mask. The felt is built up in three layers, two of felt and one of mineral felt-top.

FLAT ROOF STRUCTURE

THIRD FELT LAYER · SECOND FELT LAYER · FIRST FELT LAYER · DECKING · BATTEN · FURRING · RETURN JOIST · NOGGIN · JOISTS · FASCIA BOARD · FELT EAVES DRIP

Timber-framed flat roofs are often found on rear extensions, sheds and garages. Sturdy joists cross the shorter spans at intervals of about 45 cm (18 in). The ends of the joists are attached to wall plates on load-bearing walls, or set into the brickwork of an extension with metal hangers. Flat roofs aren't completely level: they must be slightly sloped to allow rainwater to run off. If the slope isn't sufficient, standing water can seep through. Roofers achieve this slight slope by nailing long, tapered 'furrings' to the top edges of the joists, meaning that the roof slopes a little but the ceiling inside is flat – clever! Decking lies on top of the sloping wooden framework: a simple plywood or pre-felted chipboard layer about 18 mm (¾ in) thick is nailed to the joists, providing a flat surface for the layers of roofing felt. The short lengths of wood between the joists are called 'noggins' and give extra support to the edges. Sometimes a layer of light-coloured stone or chippings is placed on top of the final layer of roofing felt in order to provide extra weatherproofing and reflect the sun's rays, lowering the temperature inside the building.

✳ DISCOVER A WHOLE NEW MEANING TO 'GETTING HAMMERED'!

Claw hammer

IT'S A TOUGH PROBLEM THAT CAN'T BE CRACKED WITH A HAMMER!

1 Apply a strip of felt one-third the width of the roll all round and over the built-up edges of the roof. Cover the decking with the remaining strips of two-thirds width, then use whole widths. Overlap each piece by 10 cm (4 in). Nail through the centre of the overlaps, then trim the edge flush to the eaves. Cut a strip of felt and wrap it around the eaves to form a 'drip' covering the edge. Snip and fold neatly at the corners, then nail into place.

2 For the second layer, cut enough pieces of felt to fit the width of the roof and glue them to the first layer using cold bitumen adhesive applied with a brush. Overlap each piece, fold and tuck around the built-up edges, then add a drip to the eaves. To glue the pieces down, put them in position and roll up half of the strip, apply the adhesive to the first layer, unroll and press flat, then roll up the other half and glue in the same way.

3 Cut and lay the mineral felt-top layer in the same way as the second layer, but lap it over the eaves drips rather than the built-up edges. Finally, cut mineral felt-top strips and nail and glue them in place round the sides and rear edges.

need

* rolls of roofing felt
* mineral felt-top layer
* ladder
* claw hammer
* galvanized roofing nails
* cold bitumen adhesive
* gloves
* mask
* Stanley knife
* soft flat-soled shoes
* lots of strong bags for the old roofing felt

SURE I'D LOVE TO HELP, BUT I MIGHT RUIN MY NICE NEW CARDI!

REPAIRING

SPLITS AND CRACKS

Localized splits and cracks can easily be fixed by applying some self-adhesive, roof-repair tape. Clear the roof of any dirt or debris first and use a fungicide to get rid of moss or algae. If the crack is quite long, stick one end of the tape to the roof and unroll the tape, pressing down as you go. As an added precaution, a liquid waterproof treatment can be applied to the entire surface, using a roller with an extended handle. Three coats will give a good weatherproof layer. Try to check the roof once or twice a year. Remove debris and wash away any mould. Note areas in which water is accumulating; they may lead to leaks in the future.

Getting down and dirty up on the roof

CLEARING A BLOCKED GUTTER

16

A blocked gutter will eventually cause water to overflow, which in turn may lead to moisture problems in the surrounding walls. The weight of standing water in plastic guttering systems can also cause distortion over time, leading to splits and cracks.

1 Make sure that the base of the ladder is on level ground and that the top is propped solidly against the wall or roof fascia. Don't place the top of the ladder on plastic or aluminium gutters because this can cause damage. Hang your bucket from one of the top rungs using a paint-kettle hook, leaving both hands free.

2 Block the gutter outlet with old rags so that the blockage doesn't fall into the downpipe instead! Inspect the gutter along its length to locate the blockages. Clear any stubborn accumulations with a trowel or plastic scraper.

RUNNING OUTLET

GUTTER

GUTTER

UNION

GUTTER CLIP

JOINT BRACKET

END STOP

ELBOWS

PIPE CLIP

PIPE

PIPE CLIP

PIPE CONNECTOR

PIPE

AND YOU CAN STILL LOOK AT THE STARS!

A BASIC GUTTERING SYSTEM

☞ Guttering can be round, square or rectangular in shape and made from aluminium, cast iron or plastic. Because all the pieces are separate, it's possible to remove a damaged or broken portion and replace it. Gutters run along the eaves, collecting water run-off from the roof. The run-off flows through the downpipe, which is connected to the underground drain. If you need to replace a piece, then it's a good idea to know its name (*see diagram*). Some of the pieces are not symmetrical, so you'll also need to note the direction of any bends before you buy new pieces.

3 Put on your rubber gloves and scoop up the debris, placing it in the bucket. When you are satisfied that the system is free from all obstructions, remove the rags from the outlet and pour a bucket of fresh water down the pipe to flush it.

need
* rubber gloves
* ladder
* bucket
* hook

FIXING A LOOSE DOWNPIPE

After years of wear and tear, your poor old downpipe can get a bit loose and wobbly. Clips can become brittle and crack, and screws can work loose. If the pipes are not held rigidly in place, over time the joints in the downpipe can leak. Leaky downpipes cause damage to brickwork and pointing, and penetrating water will eventually give rise to serious damp problems.

1 First, locate the offending pipe clips. If a clip has worked loose and the pipe moves a lot, then it will probably have caused a few others to loosen, too. Wobble the pipe around a bit to see if they are attached firmly. Use a securely positioned ladder to gain access to the high clips. Loosen the screws with the screwdriver, then remove the old clip and discard – do not try to reuse an old clip.

TIP
You can fit a plastic leaf-guard to the top of a downpipe to keep out leaves and discourage birds from setting up home there.

✳ WHEN I FIX YOUR PIPE CLIPS, THEY STAY FIXED!

WALL PLUGS

👉 Screws won't hold fast in solid masonry or brick. If you just drill a hole and insert the screw, then it will work loose and come out again in no time. You need to use wall plugs. These are tubes of plastic that are inserted into the pre-drilled screw hole. When the screw is driven in, the tube expands, gripping the inside of the hole and holding the screw secure. Choose a plug to match the size of screw you're using. Check the manufacturer's guidelines first.

Wall plugs

2 It might be necessary to replace the wall plugs if they are damaged. If so, just pull them out using long-nosed pliers and insert new ones of the same size into the old holes. Tap the new wall plug into place with a small hammer.

3 If the masonry has crumbled, it's a good idea to drill and plug a new hole in a slightly different position. Insert new wall plugs, then position the new clip around the downpipe, aligning the holes with the wall-plug holes, and screw securely in place.

need
✳ new pipe clip
✳ screws to fit
✳ screwdriver
✳ new wall plugs
✳ ladder if needed
✳ drill with masonry bit if needed
✳ long-nosed pliers

Cure those leaky downpipes

REPLACING A SECTION OF DOWNPIPE

18

Splits and damaged areas in plastic downpipes can have a number of causes. Plastic is not as strong as cast iron, for example, so if a ladder is propped against a plastic pipe, it is likely to damage it. Another cause of damage is snow and ice, especially if the gutter or downpipe is blocked with debris. The standing water in the pipe can freeze and expand, causing distortion that leads to more serious problems if left unchecked.

✳ BELIEVE ME, THE RUMOURS ABOUT MY DAMAGED DOWNPIPE ARE GREATLY EXAGGERATED!

1 Use a securely positioned ladder to reach the damaged area safely. When you have found the damage in a downpipe, loosen all the pipe clips that hold it in place. Use your tool belt to hold any tools you need for the job, leaving both hands free. Remove the damaged piece and discard it; you may have to cut out a section using the hacksaw.

2 Measure the length of the replacement piece and mark it on the new pipe. Clamp the pipe securely on your workbench and saw the pipe to size. It should be easy to make a straight cut, but if you have problems, just tape a sheet of paper round the pipe, aligning the edges, and use it as a cutting guide.

TIP
It's always better to replace a broken or damaged section of pipe than to try to repair it.

need
* ladder
* new section of downpipe
* pipe connectors if necessary
* large hacksaw
* workbench
* measuring tape
* new pipe clips

You can get special paint for plastic downpipes too!

3 If you have removed a portion of a long piece of pipe, you need to slip pipe connectors on to the ends of the old pipe and slot in the new part. The connectors will form sound, watertight joints. When you are satisfied with the job, replace all the pipe clips and check once more that the pipe is securely attached to the wall.

INSTALLING A WATER BUTT

In times of increased demand, it makes sense to save every drop of water we can and use it for our thirsty gardens or potted plants when the weather is dry. A water butt or rain barrel is the obvious way to save natural rainwater; the run-off from the roof amounts to a huge volume of water over time. These containers are available in various sizes.

1 Place the water butt and stand in a firm and level position near the downpipe and remove the lid. Make one mark on the pipe at the same height as the top of the water butt; you can use a spirit level for this. Make a second mark 10–12.5 cm (4 in–5 in) above the first, depending on the downpipe diameter. The instructions will indicate the correct measurement.

2 Use a hacksaw to cut the downpipe carefully along the lines marked. Remove the cut-out section and discard it. Try the diverter for size in the downpipe and cut where indicated in the instructions, using the Stanley knife to fit.

Make sure that you position the water butt in a cool, shady place; if it gets warm the water will evaporate.

HOW BIG DO YOU WANT YOUR BUTT TO BE, MA'AM?

3 Place the top section of the diverter in the downpipe threaded-side down, then slide the pipe up a little and hold it in position. Place the lower section in position threaded-side up. Screw the assembly together and then allow the unit to fall into the lower part of the downpipe.

4 Cut a 2.5-cm (1-in) diameter hole in the side of the water butt, placing the top of the hole about 12.5 cm (5 in) below the top of the butt. Fit the connector washer and nut to the butt, then join the diverter to the butt with the flexible hose provided.

need

* large hacksaw
* marker pen and spirit level
* measuring tape
* rainwater diverter kit
* Stanley knife
* water butt and stand

Cleaning exterior walls with style

USING A PRESSURE WASHER **20**

All you need is a power supply and a water supply. Attach your hose to an outdoor (or indoor) tap, then attach the other end to the washer. Plug the unit into an electrical socket using an outdoor extension lead. Turn on the water, then the power and off you go. The washer nozzle is adjustable, so you can have a fine jet or a spray. Hold the nozzle about 20–25 cm (8–10 in) away from the dirty surface for the best results.

need
* pressure washer
* hosepipe
* wellingtons
* rubber gloves
* fungicidal solution

ONCE YOU START, YOU WON'T BE ABLE TO STOP!

1 Rendered and painted portions of exterior walls accumulate dirt and mud splashes from rain and human or motor traffic. These eyesores are easily removed with a pressure washer. Just blast away the dirt, grime and peeling paint, then repaint when dry.

2 Here, the brickwork around a leaky downpipe has become damp and acquired a mould growth. If left untreated this would spread. Remove the mould with a pressure washer, then apply a fungicidal solution with a brush or sponge. After four hours, rinse the area with clean water – and don't forget to repair the leaky pipe!

✳ STAND BACK! ONCE I POWER UP, THERE'S NO STOPPING ME!

GETTING RID OF EFFLORESCENCE **21**

☞ Efflorescence occurs when salts in the bricks gradually migrate to the surface as the wall dries. Wearing a dust mask, brush the affected area with a dry, stiff scrubbing brush. Eventually all the salts will have been expelled from the brickwork and the problem will disappear. Be careful not to use excessive pressure if the brick surface is delicate, because this can cause damage.

need
* stiff scrubbing brush
* dust mask

USING CHEMICAL PRODUCTS

While you're in exterior clean-up mode, you might discover that a previous occupant has been a bit careless and dripped paint on the brickwork. Annoying, but not irreversible. Careful application of an ordinary paint stripper will do the trick, leaving your brickwork nice and clean. Bear this in mind if you decide to repaint the exterior. Try not to splash paint around in a haphazard fashion — it just makes more work for you to do later on.

1 Wearing your rubber gloves, decant some paint stripper into a paint kettle. Use a small paintbrush to apply the product, dabbing it into the surface thoroughly. Wait for about ten minutes or as the manufacturer directs.

* I MAY BE STRONGER, BUT SHE'S BETTER AT STRIPPING!

TIP

Paint strippers are highly toxic and give off unpleasant fumes. It is best to wear a mask when using these products.

2 The chemical stripper will dissolve and soften the paint until it is ready for removal. Remove thick residues with a paint scraper and scrub smaller areas using an old toothbrush. Repeat the process if any paint particles are left in crevices or buried deep in textured surfaces. It's worth taking time to make sure that all the paint particles are removed.

need
* paint stripper
* paint kettle
* rubber gloves
* paintbrush
* old toothbrush
* scrubbing brush
* paint scraper

SAFETY

☞ Never direct the washer jet at people or animals.

☞ Always wear protective gloves when using paint-stripping products because they are extremely caustic and will burn you if they come into contact with your skin.

3 Finally, when you are satisfied, rinse the whole area with clean water. Use a bucket and a scrubbing brush, or a hosepipe if you can. Try not to leave any paint particles on the brick surface. When all is dry, give the brickwork a scrub with a dry brush.

Pointing in the right direction

SIMPLE BRICK REPOINTING

The shaping of the mortar joints between bricks is known as pointing. Over time these joints can crumble and become porous, allowing water to penetrate the brickwork, which in turn can give rise to dampness that can freeze in cold conditions and cause further damage. You can undertake a small repointing task yourself. Doing the whole house is a job for the pros!

1. Rake out all the old and damaged mortar. Place the point of a plugging chisel on the mortar and tap it with a club hammer. Remember to wear gloves and goggles when you do this. Brush away any small particles with a stiff brush.

need

* plugging chisel
* club hammer
* gloves and goggles
* stiff brush
* trowel
* ready-mixed dry mortar
* water
* mortar board
* Frenchman

TIP

Don't overwater the mortar mixture, because this can weaken it. It needs to be wet enough to be workable, but not sloppy.

2. Mix a small amount of mortar on a mortar board (or a sheet of stiff, flat board). Place a small heap of dry mortar in the middle of the board and make a well in the centre. Pour a little cold water into the well and mix with the trowel. Add water little by little until the mortar reaches a workable consistency.

Don't start pointing if it looks like it's going to rain; you'll get wet and the mortar will be slow to set!

3. Scoop up thin, sausage-shaped wedges of mortar on the back of the trowel and push them quickly and firmly into the vertical joints. This is quite tricky, but fun. The aim is to fill the gap completely without smearing the mortar all over the rest of the brickwork.

4. When all the vertical joints are filled, it's time to fill the horizontal joints. Do this in the same way. The shape of the mortar filling doesn't matter too much at this stage.

MORTAR JOINT SHAPES

There are different ways to finish mortar joints. A flush joint is rubbed with a stiff brush to bring out the sand aggregate in the mortar. A raked joint emphasizes the bonding pattern of a wall and is achieved by scraping out the mortar with a thin wooden lath. This is not suitable for walls that are exposed to heavy weather. A concave joint is curved in profile; simply run a small piece of pipe along the mortar joint to create the shape, or use a mortar shaper. The sloping shape of weatherstruck joints directs water downwards and away from the wall.

FLUSH JOINT	RAKED JOINT	CONCAVE JOINT	WEATHERSTRUCK JOINT

5 Use the point of the trowel to shape the mortar joints (*see above*). Do the verticals first, then the horizontals. Slide the trowel along the joints from top to bottom on the verticals and along each horizontal in turn.

6 Use your Frenchman to scoop up the bits of mortar that have been squeezed out by the pointing process. It is important to do this quickly because the mortar soon dries, and then you'll have a problem removing it. Hold the mortar board or trowel under the work area to catch falling blobs of mortar.

MAKING A FRENCHMAN

☞ C'est magnifique! The Frenchman is a very nifty tool for scraping excess mortar away from joints when a pointing job is complete (*see left*). You can make one easily by heating the blade of an old kitchen knife in the flame of a blowtorch or gas cooker; when it's hot and malleable, bend the knife at right angles using a pair of pliers. Alternatively, you can make one from a strip of thin metal such as aluminium. The strip needs to be about 20 cm x 2.5 cm (8 in x 1 in). Bend the end at right angles, then bind a portion of the straight part with masking tape to make a handle.

Frenchman

Now for the fun part — choosing colours

PRIMING AND PAINTING EXTERIOR WALLS

24

So you've decided to paint your exterior because you fancy a new colour or the old paint finish is looking a bit sad? Make sure that you have a few days in which to complete the task. Ideally the weather should be dry and warm but overcast. Masonry paint can be smooth or textured; simply decide which you prefer. Here comes the hard part — the colour! Grab some colour charts and take your pick. Just remember that you must use exterior-grade masonry paint: interior paint won't do (although the colour range is better…).

need

* extending ladder
* stiff brush
* fungicide
* exterior surface stabilizer
* exterior paint
* 10-cm or 15-cm (4-in or 6-in) paintbrush
* narrow paintbrush
* gloves and goggles
* bucket and sponge
* paint kettle
* dust sheets
* newspaper
* masking tape
* mask

LADDER SAFETY

When using any kind of access equipment, safety is of the utmost importance (*see page 19*). Always make sure that the foot of the ladder is secured to the ground and that it leans against the wall at a safe angle, ideally about 70 degrees. There should never be more than one person up the ladder at any one time, and while you're on it, don't stretch out sideways: if you can't reach comfortably, move the ladder.

CALCULATING PAINT QUANTITIES

In general, paints will have an indication of the coverage area on the tin. Simply calculate the approximate surface area of your house (i.e. multiply the height by the width of all the sides to be painted, then add all the figures together) and divide by the amount on the tin.

Masonry paintbrush

TIP

Decant paint into a paint kettle and hang it from a ladder rung with a paint-kettle hook. If you're finishing off an old tin of paint, strain it through muslin into the kettle – it may contain lumps of dirt or rust.

ORDER OF WORK

☞ It pays to have a good plan of action when starting a big paint job like the front of a house. Use the numbered diagram above as a guide. Always apply paint to complete sections in turn; never stop painting halfway across a large area because this will show when the paint is dry. Use downpipes as natural breaks, so that you aren't left with obvious stop-start lines. Cover the ground with dust sheets to protect it from paint splashes and falling paint kettles or tins. Paint the walls first, then paint the window frames and doors.

TIP
Try using a long-handled roller to reach areas from ground level.

1 Spend time preparing the walls before painting. Use a stiff scrubbing brush to remove flakes of old paint and dirt. If green moss or mould is a problem, clean the surfaces thoroughly and brush the affected area with fungicide. Leave it for twenty-four hours and then hose down the walls with clean water. Allow them to dry completely before painting.

2 While the walls are drying, prepare the surrounding area by covering it with dust sheets. Take some sheets of newspaper and wrap them around all the downpipes, holding them in place with strips of masking tape. This takes all the stress out of painting behind them; simply remove the paper when the painting is completed.

3 Make any repairs – such as filling cracks – now and allow the filler to dry before continuing. If you find that the surface of the wall is chalky, apply a coat of a stabilizing primer. These products are usually colourless, but they are also available in white, which is quite an advantage if you're thinking of a colour change. This one looks blue when wet but loses its colour when dry.

4 Everything is now ready for painting. Use a large masonry paintbrush; if a rendered wall is highly textured, then you will need to use a stippling action, jabbing the brush against the surface to ensure good paint coverage. A roller can be used for smooth surfaces, but in general, rollers and paint trays are a bit of a nightmare when you're up a ladder. Use a narrower brush for awkward corners and when painting round door and window frames.

I ALWAYS LIKE TO DRESS FOR THE OCCASION!

Repairing small cracks in walls

PATCHING EXTERIOR WALLS

Exterior walls are sometimes covered with cement render, the surface of which can be smooth or slightly textured. The insulation properties of such an outer coating are clear, but you can be sure that small holes and cracks will form from time to time because of the weather. Any damage must be repaired as soon as you notice it — before things get out of hand and before any redecoration can be undertaken. Small cracks are easily repaired, but if you find that large chunks of render are falling off, then you should consider calling in a professional. Applying render to a large area is definitely not a job to do yourself.

need

* cold chisel
* club hammer
* trowel
* filling knife
* exterior filler
* old paintbrush
* stiff brush

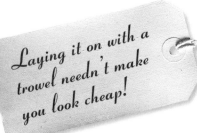

Laying it on with a trowel needn't make you look cheap!

1 Rake out the crack in the surface of the render. Place the point of a cold chisel at the start of the crack and gently tap it with a club hammer to remove any loose or crumbling render – don't hack off big chunks. Brush away any dust with a large paintbrush.

2 Dampen the area surrounding the crack with some water: wet the bristles of a paintbrush and dab lightly. The render surface needs to be damp, not soaked – the moisture helps the filler adhere properly to the surface.

3 Use a filling knife or trowel to fill the crack with exterior filler. For long, thin cracks, fill with a caulking gun. To match a smooth-finished render, allow the patch to dry and rub it smooth with abrasive paper.

4 If the surrounding surface is textured, apply a thinner layer of filler to the repair when it is dry and then use a stiff brush to texture it while it is still a bit soft. Repaint when completely dry.

EXTERIOR TIMBER CLADDING

☞ Exterior timber cladding consists of overlapping planks that are nailed to battens or underlying sheathing. Because they overlap, rather than interlock, it is easy to replace a small damaged section.

need

* crowbar
* tenon saw
* chisel
* mini hacksaw
* try square
* pencil
* wooden wedges
* hammer
* nails
* new piece of cladding
* protective batten
* exterior wood filler
* abrasive paper

1 Mark lines on either side of the damaged area using a pencil, try square and saw. The lines must be at right angles to the edge of the board. Use the crowbar to ease the damaged board out so that you can slide two wedges underneath (just beyond the damaged area) to keep it raised.

2 Drive a thin piece of wood under the board where a saw line is marked. Use the tenon saw to cut along the line and a hammer and chisel to finish the cut, because it will be difficult to saw all the way through. Cut along the second line in the same way.

3 Remove the damaged part in one piece if you can, but if this is hard, then you may have to break it into pieces carefully. Old nails might also hinder your progress. If you find any passing through the board above, cut through them using a mini hacksaw. Slide the blade under the board, cut through the nail and remove it as gently as possible.

4 Cut the new piece of board to fit the gap you have created. The fit will have to be exact, so measure across the top and the bottom of the gap just in case there are slight differences. Position the new piece between the cut ends of the old board, then place a batten along the lower edge and tap it home with a hammer.

5 When you are satisfied that the new piece fits perfectly you can nail or screw it securely in place. Fill the nail holes and joints at the ends of the board with an exterior-quality wood filler and sand them smooth when they are dry. Apply a coat or two of paint so that the repair matches the rest of the cladding.

Yes, it's time to use the pressure washer again!

CLEANING UPVC OR METAL CLADDING

27

You have to admit that UPVC or metal cladding is pretty tough, low-maintenance stuff. However, it's there on the outside of your house, exposed to the elements all year round, and you know what that means — dirt! Eventually it will require a good cleaning. It's best to do this job regularly to keep the exterior looking good.

USING THE PRESSURE WASHER

Hey, it's the wonderful pressure washer again! This cool machine is just the ticket for cleaning cladding. The water jet reaches all the nooks, crannies and convoluted surfaces in which dirt and residue can collect. Don't do this on a very windy day because the water will just blow everywhere. Remember to wear wellies and rubber gloves, as this is a pretty wet job.

OPERATING INSTRUCTIONS

Do you keep instruction manuals for all your tools and equipment in a safe place? I do. This is not obsessive behaviour; it makes good sense if you use a piece of equipment frequently (and if you have a pressure washer then you certainly will). Refer to the manual for full connection and operating instructions and maintenance procedures.

CLEANING BY HAND

Oh, dear! No pressure washer? Use a nice soft cloth and a big bucket of soapy water. This method is a little more time-consuming but it does the job eventually. It is most important not to use a brush or any kind of abrasive on metal or UPVC cladding because this can scratch the surface.

need
* pressure washer
* rubber gloves
* wellingtons
* bucket
* cloth

DON'T MAKE ME ANGRY. YOU WOULDN'T LIKE ME WHEN I'M ANGRY!

THE FORCE IS STRONG IN THIS ONE, PRINCESS!

TIP
Plain water is usually sufficient for normal cleaning, but now and then a cleaning solution will come in useful. You can feed the solution through the pressure washer using a bottle attached to the hose.

Pressure Washer

RENOVATING TIMBER CLADDING

Occasionally, a portion of your timber cladding will rot or sustain damage. The only remedy is to remove it and replace it with a matching piece (*see page 75*). Small areas of damage, such as holes, can be repaired easily with an epoxy wood filler. Simply apply the filler, allow it to dry, sand smooth and repaint. When a timber cladding board splits, it is not always necessary to remove the damaged part and replace it. Try this easy repair.

need

* waterproof wood glue
* chisel
* hammer
* nails
* cloth

1 Locate the split board and place the chisel blade gently inside the split at the end of the board. Carefully hold the crack open (you can use a thin wooden wedge for this) while you squeeze some wood glue into it, covering both sides liberally.

2 Allow the wood to spring back into the original position. Press the glued edges together tightly and secure the board to the batten or sheathing underneath with nails or screws. Use a damp cloth to wipe away any excess glue.

TYPES OF TIMBER CLADDING

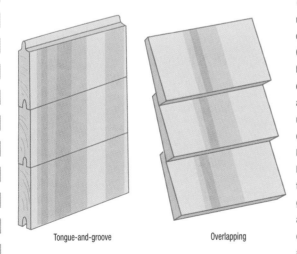

Tongue-and-groove   Overlapping

👉 Timber cladding is available in many different profiles including overlapping and tongue-and-groove. Overlapping boards are nailed to studs, battens or sheathing underneath and can be removed individually. Tongue-and-groove boards are interlocked, so removing them is more difficult. The damaged board must be cut across and lengthwise to facilitate removal. Usually, boards are fixed horizontally, making them easy to get out, but tongue-and-groove boards may be set at an angle and used to create small panels outlined by wide flat boards. These are not so easy to repair.

WHEN PAINTING WOODEN CLADDING, BEGIN AT THE TOP AND WORK DOWNWARDS.

Keeping your walls and brickwork watertight

29

APPLYING SEALANTS AND WATERPROOFING

Sealants can be applied to just about any surface you can imagine in order to repel moisture, dirt, oil and grease. In addition, mastic compounds can be used to weatherproof joints between adjacent surfaces. Check out all the fabulous products that are available these days. There's only one golden rule: clean the surface thoroughly first! There's no point in applying a sealant to a dirty surface because you'll just seal the dirt in, which is not a good idea. Weatherproof and seal garage floors, driveway walls, flat roofs, window frames, patios, exterior wood, furniture…you name it.

Most sealant products are liquid, dry with a clear finish and can be applied easily with a brush or roller.

TIP
Exterior woodwork or furniture can be sealed in the same way.

WALLS AND BRICKWORK

1 First, clean the surface to be treated, whether it's brick, concrete or render. Use a wire brush to remove dirt and any loose particles. This will be a dusty job so be sure to wear a dust mask. If fungal growth is a problem on your brickwork or walls, apply a coat of good fungicide following the manufacturer's instructions. Fungicide can be applied with a brush or roller.

need
* water sealant product
* rubber gloves
* wire brush
* trowel
* mortar
* large paintbrush
* paint kettle

2 Repair any damaged areas. Repoint worn or crumbling joints with a trowel as shown, and fill any cracks or holes with a suitable filler. Allow all repairs to dry completely before applying sealant.

3 Decant the sealant liquid into a small paint kettle so that it's easier to handle. If you're using a ladder, hang the kettle from one of the top rungs, leaving you with both hands free. Apply the sealant using a large brush, working from the bottom up. If the product requires a second coat, then allow adequate drying time before reapplication. Sealants are toxic, so keep the bucket and brush out of harm's way while you wait for the first application to dry.

SAFETY

☞ If using liquid sealants indoors – for example, on a garage floor – make sure that the area is adequately ventilated. The fumes given off by the sealant can be unpleasant and sometimes toxic.

☞ Wear rubber gloves; do not allow sealant products to come into contact with your skin.

☞ Wear a respirator as an added precaution to prevent the inhalation of toxic fumes.

WINDOW FRAMES

need

* exterior-grade mastic cartridge
* caulking gun
* Stanley knife

1 Insert the mastic cartridge into the gun and cut off the end of the nozzle with a craft knife. Place the nozzle against the edge of the window frame. Press the trigger to release a thin, toothpaste-like bead of mastic.

2 Run the caulking gun along all four sides of the window frame in order to create a sound, watertight seal. Most mastics set quite quickly and can be painted within a few hours. The beauty of mastic is that it doesn't set hard, it remains flexible. Remember to clean the frame and surrounding surfaces before sealing.

Caulking guns are great for sealing small gaps.

* I USUALLY STORE MY SEALANT GUN ON THE LEFT!

PATIOS AND PATHS

☞ Exterior floors like patios are subject to dirty feet, barbecue leftovers and mould, as well as adverse weather conditions. Driveways and garage floors have oil spills and drips to contend with. Follow these easy steps and you'll have a pristine surface in no time.

1 Brush away loose debris, then use a patio cleaner with the same brush to remove dirt and mould. Scrub the surface briskly and leave it for about ten minutes. Hose it down with clean water and let dry.

BLOCK PAVERS

2 Block-paver sealant products are designed to penetrate deep into the surface of the blocks, drying with a highly durable, clear finish. The result is a surface that repels water, stains, oil and grease, and is resistant to fungal growth, too. Apply two coats using a long-handled roller, allowing at least four hours drying time between coats.

PAVING SLABS

need

* wellingtons
* rubber gloves
* floor brush
* bucket
* patio and paving cleaner
* hosepipe
* patio sealer
* block-paver sealer
* roller with long handle
* roller tray

2 Paving-slab patios can be sealed to give a waterproof, stain-resistant surface, which will also resist weather damage. Clean as in step 1 and apply a coat of sealant using a long-handled roller. Apply a second coat after two hours. Use a quick-drying product to ensure that the patio is ready for use in the minimum time.

Simple repairs for cracked or broken windows

REGLAZING A WINDOW

From time to time, window panes will break or crack and will need to be replaced. This can be due to many things, from stray footballs to severe weather conditions. If you are able to remove the window from the frame, then do so and make the repair indoors; if not, do it with the window in place. While it's a fairly simple matter to replace a small or medium-sized pane, anything larger than about 1 m (3 ft) should be left to a professional glazier. Glass is dangerous to handle at the best of times, so it's best not to risk having an accident with a large pane.

1 First, with gloved hands, remove any pieces of broken glass. Then, using a chisel and the side of a hammer, remove all the putty. Put the blade of the chisel on the putty and gently tap the handle. If the putty is really old and hard, try softening it up with a blast from a heat gun. With a bit of luck, you will be able to scrape the putty away with a knife.

2 When the putty has been removed, you'll probably see a few triangular glazing sprigs protruding from the frame. These are used to hold the glass pane in place. Pull them out carefully using long-nosed pliers. Make sure the rebate (the recess along the edge of the frame) is clean and smooth; sand it if necessary.

3 Take a small amount of putty in your hand and roll it into a really skinny sausage. Place the putty sausage into the corner of the rebate all round. This creates a watertight seal between the glass and the frame.

❋ MY, HER WINDOWS ARE ALMOST AS BRIGHT AND SHINY AS OUR TEETH!

❋ LET'S HOPE THEY ARE FIXED IN AS FIRMLY!

4 Cut a 20-cm (8-in) strip of duct tape and pinch the centre together a bit to make a T-shape. Attach the sticky parts to the centre of the glass. Pick up the glass with gloved hands and place it into the frame. Use the tape 'handle' to ease it into position.

5 Use the chisel or putty knife to tap glazing sprigs into the rebate all around to hold the pane in place. Take some more putty and roll it into a fatter sausage, about 1.2 cm (½ in) in diameter. Squeeze small lumps of putty from the sausage all round the four sides of the pane using your forefinger.

need
* gloves and safety goggles
* new pane cut to size by glazier
* hammer and chisel
* heat gun
* long-nosed pliers
* glazing sprigs
* duct tape
* putty
* putty knife

Wipe off stray putty while it's wet or it'll stick to the glass.

WASHING WINDINGS 31

WINDOWS

👉 Use a small paintbrush to clear dirt from the corners of the window frames. Fill the bucket with soapy water and get to work with a cloth or sponge. Rinse with clean water using a chamois-leather cloth or even a sheet of scrunched-up newspaper (the grease in the printing ink makes the glass shine). You want the easy option? Give the windows a blast with the pressure washer and have some fun at the same time!

6 Use the putty knife to smooth out the putty; it has a forty-five-degree-angled part specifically designed for this purpose. Allow the putty to dry, then prime and repaint the window to match the others. Don't paint over damp putty – the paint finish will be ruined.

Stanley knife

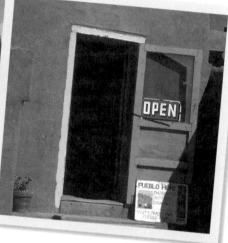

Learn how to be

a screen queen

MENDING SCREEN DOORS AND WINDOWS

Screening, whether aluminium or fibreglass, is not indestructible. Small tears in both types can be mended by dabbing a little silicone glue on to the tear. Aluminium screening can be 'darned'; just unravel a few strands from a spare piece of mesh and use a needle to weave them over the tear. Both types can be patched: use glue for fibreglass or ready-made repair patches for aluminium. These have pre-hooked edges that clip on to the surrounding mesh. If the screen has sustained damage in several areas, then it's best to replace the screen completely — just follow the steps opposite.

SCREEN DOORS COME IN A VARIETY OF DECORATIVE YET FUNCTIONAL STYLES – AND SMALL REPAIRS ARE VERY EASY.

need

* screwdriver
* Stanley knife
* aluminium or fibreglass screening
* splining tool
* new spline

✳ I CHOSE FIBREGLASS AND LOOK AT ALL THIS MONEY I HAVE TO SPEND ON REAL SHOPPING!

Aluminium is more durable, but fibreglass is cheap and easier to install.

SPLINING TOOL

☛ You cannot replace a screen panel without a screen-installation splining tool! It looks very much like a double-ended pastry cutter with a wheel at each end. One wheel has a convex edge and is used for pushing the edge of the screening into the groove; the other wheel has a concave edge and is used to insert the rubber spline into the groove (it's the rope-like spline that keeps the screening in place). Splining tools come in two sizes, so choose one that fits the groove you have in your screen. Remember, use the right tool for the right job!

TIP

For aluminium screening, cut the new panel so it overlaps the frame by 1.2 cm (½ in). Use the concave end of the tool to insert the spline and push the mesh into the groove at the same time. Trim excess away with a Stanley knife.

❋ I'M READY
FOR MY
CLOSE-UP
NOW, MR.
DE MILLE!

❶ Remove the old rubber spline and damaged screening. Ease the spline out of the groove with a screwdriver or the point of a bradawl. If you're careful you may be able to reuse the old spline for the replacement.

❷ Wipe the groove clean. Lay the screening on the frame and cut it to size with a Stanley knife. The edges should overlap the groove by 1.2 cm (½ in). Cut each corner diagonally, just inside the outer edge of the groove.

❸ Use the convex roller of the spline tool to push the edge of the screening into the spline groove. Position the roller at a forty-five-degree angle to the inside edge of the spline groove, and hold the screen taut while you work.

❹ Use the concave end to push the spline into the groove. Negotiate the corners by bending the spline at right angles – do not cut the spline. When all sides are secured, use a Stanley knife to trim off excess screening.

Shut up and get on with it, girl!

ATTACHING DECORATIVE SHUTTERS

33

Exterior shutters can be decorative or functional; many people use them to emphasize or complement the architectural style of their homes. Traditional shutters are made of wood, which needs quite a lot of maintenance; repainting lots of shutters is a time-consuming task. Modern shutters are usually made from moulded plastic, which is easy to care for, saving you time and effort. Decorative shutters are simply mounted on brackets attached to the exterior wall, so removal is easy when it's time for spring cleaning.

need

* shutters
* drill with hammer action
* bradawl
* screwdriver
* bracket or plastic fasteners
* hammer

* I NEVER KNEW SHUTTERS COULD BE SO CHIC!

INSTALLATION

☛ Fully operational shutters are supposed to cover the window completely to protect the glass and keep out draughts. Bear this in mind when you choose the size of your decorative shutters. Even if they don't actually work, they should at least appear to be the right size for the windows in order to look authentic.

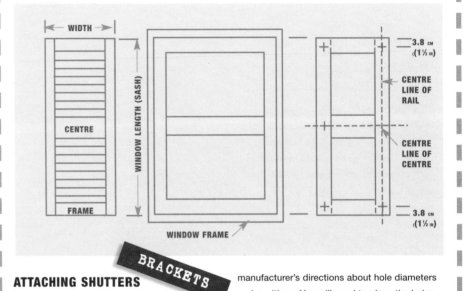

WIDTH
WINDOW LENGTH (SASH)
CENTRE
FRAME
WINDOW FRAME

3.8 cm (1½ in)
CENTRE LINE OF RAIL
CENTRE LINE OF CENTRE
3.8 cm (1½ in)

ATTACHING SHUTTERS
BRACKETS

❶ Special shutter hardware is available to facilitate easy removal. Mark the desired shutter position on either side of the window.

❷ Screw the brackets to the wall using the fittings provided. The shutter simply hangs on the bracket.

ATTACHING SHUTTERS
FASTENERS

❶ Mark the shutter positions on either side of the window: make sure that they are level with each other. Drill screw holes through the shutter frame (most will not have pre-drilled holes): one at each corner and one at the centre of both sides is usually sufficient. If you are attaching shutters to cladding, follow the manufacturer's directions about hole diameters and positions. You will need to place the holes at the highest point of the cladding to ensure that the shutter is fully supported.

❷ Reposition the shutters against the wall, and using the drilled shutter as a template, mark the positions for the screw holes on the wall with a bradawl. Make a screw hole at each point, using a twist bit for wooden cladding and a masonry bit for brick or masonry.

❸ The shutters are attached to the wall with plastic 'Christmas tree' fasteners – the ribbed shafts are designed to better grip the wall. Gently tap each fastener in using your hammer. Be careful when using the hammer if the new shutters are made of moulded plastic – one slip could cause damage to the shutter.

SOME SHUTTER STYLES

☞ Take your pick from the many shutter styles that are available. The shutters shown here would look fabulous both indoors and outdoors. Modern decorative shutters are sometimes moulded from durable, maintenance-free plastic. The colours are moulded-through and are UV-stable, so there's no paint to chip, crack or peel – simply install and admire!

Outdoor plastic shutters require very little maintenance!

TIP
Many DIY stores will have a good selection of shutters to choose from, so do a bit of price checking before you buy.

Traditional style
✻ These outdoor shutters are moulded in a traditional style with thin, open-back or closed-back louvres.

Plantation style
✻ The plantation-style shutters have wider louvres, which can be open-back or closed-back.

Raised-panel style
✻ These are solid shutters with raised panels. All styles of shutter come with an option of quarter-round arch tops.

Feel a storm brewing?

INSTALLING A STORM DOOR

A typical storm door has a glass pane or screen panel (or both) supported in a metal frame. In cold climates, a storm door will seal the main door against cold, while protecting the door itself from the elements. In warm weather, the glass panes can be replaced with screen panels so that you can open the main door without fear of insect invasion. Storm doors are easy to install; you just need to find a door to fit neatly round the opening of the existing door. Most units consist of a door with an integral mounting flange. It might also make sense to remove the glass panes, since this will make the unit lighter to handle during installation.

Draughty doors cause 40% of a building's energy losses.

need
* hammer
* drill
* screwdriver

HEY! **MOUNTING A STORM DOOR**

First of all, choose which direction you'd like the door to open – that is, should the hinges be on the left or on the right? Screw the storm door's mounting flange directly to the existing frame. Drill the screw holes first. Check that the door fits squarely within the door flange and seals tightly when closed. Attach door handles and locking mechanisms when the door is in position. The application of weatherstripping greatly reduces air leakage around the edge of the storm door.

STORM-DOOR MOUNTING FLANGE

STORM DOOR

EXISTING DOOR

STORM-DOOR CATCH

DOOR CASING

STORM DOOR

EXISTING DOOR

DOOR CASING

STORM-DOOR MOUNTING FLANGE

INSTALLING STORM WINDOWS

Gone are the days when exterior shutters were used to protect windows from damage during storms — instead, try installing combination storm windows. Measure all your windows accurately and have the units custom-built to fit. Try each unit in its intended position and trim the edges a little with tin snips to ensure a perfect fit. Aluminium storm windows usually have ribbed flanges to make trimming easy. Always trim off a little at a time and check the fit after each adjustment. You can always trim more off, but you can't put it back!

TIP
Take measurements in three places: top, middle and bottom, then use the smallest one as a guide when ordering custom-built windows.

1 When you are satisfied with the fit of each unit, clean the window frame. Apply a bead of silicone mastic around the perimeter of the existing frame where the flanges of the new window will make contact.

2 Carefully lift each unit into position. Work around the edge, pressing the flange firmly so it makes contact with the mastic underneath. The mastic creates a watertight seal. Wipe away excess with a damp cloth.

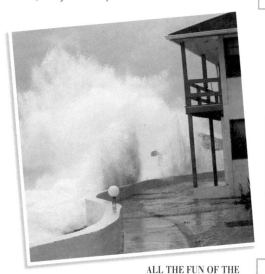

ALL THE FUN OF THE STORM AND NONE OF THE MESS, THANKS TO YOUR NEW STORM WINDOWS!

3 You can now screw your new combination storm windows securely to the existing window frames. Custom-built units will usually include screws with heads that match the flange, so the hardware will be as unobtrusive as possible.

QUIT MESSING WITH THOSE WINDOWS, LADY, AND COME HELP ME GET DRESSED!

need
* drill
* screwdriver
* tin snips
* caulking gun with exterior-grade mastic cartridge

Make a grand entrance

REPAINTING AN EXTERIOR DOOR

36

Exterior woodwork looks lovely when freshly painted, but every year Mother Nature sends a whole lot of lousy weather that doesn't bode well for paint finishes in the long term. I'm afraid, girls, that every few years you'll have to rub down and repaint the woodwork if you want your exterior to look great. Anyway, it's a good excuse to change the colour, and that can't be bad, can it?

✳ WHAT GIRL DOESN'T APPRECIATE A GORGEOUS NEW COAT EVERY NOW AND THEN?

need

* sander
* dust mask
* screwdriver
* cloth
* bucket
* gloves
* exterior wood filler
* filling knife
* masking tape
* paintbrush
* primer, if wood is bare
* self-priming exterior gloss paint
* clear gloss exterior varnish

❶ First, unscrew and remove the door handles and any other fittings. Remember to keep the spindle on your side of the door or you'll find yourself locked out if it slams shut! Wash all the woodwork and the threshold with soapy water to remove dirt and grease.

❷ Examine the frame thoroughly for cracks in the wood or small imperfections in the surface. Using a filling knife with a flexible blade, fill all damaged areas so that they are flush with the surrounding timber. Wait until the filler has set completely. For large holes or deep cracks, apply the filler in thin layers, allowing each to dry before applying the next.

❸ Use an electric sander to rub down all the surfaces until they are completely smooth, including the threshold. You could use abrasive paper for this, but it really is hard work and I would recommend that you save yourself a bit of time and effort! Remember to wear a dust mask when sanding.

4 Mask off the edges of the glass panes with strips of masking tape. It is worth taking time to do this properly, because it protects the glass so you don't need to be so careful around the edges. Otherwise you'll be scraping the paint off the glass later.

WEATHERBOARD

DOOR-STOP

DOOR

WEATHERBOARD MOULDING

SILL

DRIP GROOVE

☞ The weatherboard is a moulded strip of wood fitted across the bottom of an inward-opening external door. The purpose of the board is to make a weatherproof seal at the bottom of the door, deflecting rainwater away from the threshold underneath, and also to keep wind and rain from coming in through the door.

YOU MAY COME ACROSS SOME OF THESE PROBLEMS!

PAINT TROUBLE

☞ Peeling paint: the wood underneath is damp, dirty or greasy, causing the top coat to lift, or the top coat was applied over flaky paint.

☞ Wrinkling paint: the top coat was applied too thickly, causing it to sag. Two thin coats are much better than one thick one.

☞ Cracking paint: a network of cracks appears if the top coat is applied before the undercoat is dry, or if the two coats are incompatible.

☞ Blistering paint: usually caused by trapped solvent vapour underneath the skin of paint or moisture escaping from the wood. Sometimes blistering can be caused by exposure to strong sunlight, resulting in large, unsightly paint bubbles.

5 Stir the paint well before application. I used a self-priming exterior gloss paint suitable for wood and metal. This is a wonderful time-saver because there's no need to prime. However, if the wood is completely bare, I would advise that you prime first.

6 Now for the threshold. This is a piece of wood that is permanently fixed across the entrance to the door and which acts as a weather barrier (and trips you up occasionally if you forget it's there). Apply one or two coats of an exterior-quality, clear gloss varnish to seal and waterproof the wood, allowing the necessary drying time between applications. Pay special attention to the threshold because this gets the worst of the rain.

Give your *UPVC* a little *TLC*

RENOVATING AND PAINTING UPVC WINDOWS

37

UPVC windows are relatively low-maintenance. No wooden frame to rot, warp or take care of, and they're double-glazed, too. However, plastic doesn't stay clean for ever. So what's the answer? Manufacturers have now come up with specially formulated products that stick to plastic window frames. They are non-yellowing and contain fungicides to protect against mould. So you can now return your windows to their former glory and in any colour, too!

These paints are low in volatile organic compounds, so they're not so bad for the environment.

1 Clean the window frame with warm soapy water or a special UPVC cleaner – the adhesion of the product relies on a spotlessly clean surface. Do not use a scrubbing brush or any abrasive because this will scratch the surface.

2 When the cleaning is done, take some time to mask off the edges of the glass on all four sides of each unit using strips of masking tape. This just makes your job a bit easier: the tape protects the glass from the paint so that you don't have to be so careful when painting round the edges. Peel off the tape when the painting is complete.

3 Stir the paint well and apply one even coat of UPVC gloss (or primer if changing colour). Use a synthetic brush suitable for water-based paint for the best results. Recoat after eight hours for gloss and four for primer.

4 When the first coat of paint or primer is dry, sand off any imperfections with fine abrasive paper and wipe away dust using a damp cloth. Apply the top coat of white or the first coat of coloured gloss paint and allow to dry. If you've taken the colourful option, you will probably need to apply another coat when the first is dry. Now clean your brushes with soapy water.

need

* UPVC cleaner
* soft cloth
* rubber gloves
* masking tape
* paintbrush
* abrasive paper
* UPVC primer (if changing colour)
* UPVC brilliant white gloss (or exterior gloss in a colour)

TAKING CARE OF YOUR DOOR FURNITURE

38

Dull or corroded door furniture is not attractive; everybody wants their knobs, knockers and handles to be nice and shiny. Metal fittings inevitably lose their shine after a while, but this can be remedied easily with a little metal polish, a soft cloth and some good old-fashioned elbow grease. If the elements have taken a severe toll on your brass door fittings, you could find yourself with an ugly brown build-up of deposits that is difficult to polish away. Take one cup of hot water, add one tablespoon each of salt and vinegar, and apply the solution liberally to the affected item using a pad of fine wire wool. This will soften the deposits nicely; just rinse them with water, dry and polish.

1 Put on your rubber gloves and mix up the solution in a small container. Take a short length of fine wire wool and roll it into a small pad. Apply the solution liberally to the brass fitting, working it into the surface with small circular movements. If possible, unscrew the fittings and do this on a table. If this is too difficult, do it with the fittings in place.

2 After a little while, you will see the nasty deposits dissolving before your eyes. When the brass looks clean, wash it with warm soapy water and rinse thoroughly with clean water. Dry it with a clean cloth.

3 Now put your backs into it, girls. Polish the brass, using a lot of elbow grease, a soft cloth and a little metal polish. It really doesn't take that long to do and the difference is remarkable. Better than buying new ones!

AND WHEN YOU'VE FINISHED THAT, YOU CAN BUFF UP MY SHINY NEW BOOTS!

need
* rubber gloves
* plastic basin
* fine wire wool
* soft cloth
* salt
* vinegar
* metal polish

TIP
If you have brass numbers on your door, unscrew and submerge them in the salt-and-vinegar solution for a while before drying and polishing.

Keep railings looking gorgeous

RENOVATING CAST-IRON RAILINGS

Cast-iron railings are a wonderful feature, unless they're dirty and in need of a bit of cosmetic attention. Follow these simple steps to renovate any kind of exterior metalwork, including cast-iron downpipes, gates and all sorts of decorative metal structures. Check out your DIY store for special metal paints and primers for galvanized steel and aluminium surfaces. Paint manufacturers are developing great new products all the time.

❋ I JUST LOVE SHINY THINGS, DON'T YOU?

❶ Put on a dust mask before you begin. Use the wire brush to remove loose paint flakes, rust particles and any fungal growths. Brush in all directions so that you don't miss any intricate or convoluted areas. Be extra careful when cleaning paintwork that dates back to 1960 or earlier, because it may contain harmful lead. It is a good idea to do a job like this on a day with little or no wind – otherwise the paint particles and dust will blow everywhere.

❷ Sand all surfaces with coarse abrasive paper, taking the shine off the previous paintwork and creating a good base for the primer and top coats. Roll the abrasive paper into a small tube to get into small, tight or curved areas. Use a flexible sanding pad on intricately patterned surfaces.

❸ Use a specially formulated metal cleaner/de-greaser to clean the railings thoroughly. Metal can be a tricky surface to paint, so make it as easy on yourself as possible. Simply spray the cleaning product on to all the surfaces.

need

* rubber gloves
* dust mask
* paintbrushes
* bucket
* exterior metal primer
* exterior metal paint
* white spirit for cleaning up
* abrasive paper
* wire brush
* cloth
* metal cleaner/ de-greaser
* rust stabilizer

4 Fill the bucket with warm soapy water. Wash the railings down to remove all residues and allow to dry completely. If you've discovered rust patches, apply a rust stabilizer to the affected area and allow it to dry. Follow the directions on the product package; application with a small brush will usually suffice. It's just as important to treat small areas because rust will spread.

5 Using a clean brush, apply a liberal coat of primer and allow it to dry. If you do not intend to change the colour of the metal, you can skip this stage and move directly to the top coat. Do a job like this on a warm, dry day; in windy weather, dust particles can blow on to the wet surface – then you'll have to sand and repaint.

6 Finally, when the primer is dry, apply one or two coats of paint. Always allow the necessary drying time between paint applications. If you are changing the colour, two coats are advisable. In this case it is best to apply the paint in thick coats to provide a protective layer.

The colour range for exterior paints is getting broader all the time.

❋ MARRY ME, ALICE, AND WE CAN PAINT BEAUTIFUL RAILINGS TOGETHER!

TIP
Use plenty of old newspaper to protect the surrounding area from drips.

DON'T FORGET TO TAKE THE CHAMPAGNE OUT FIRST!

Turning on the waterworks outside

INSTALLING AN OUTDOOR TAP

40

A tap on an outside wall is a real advantage when it comes to pressure-washing exteriors or watering the garden. The only other alternative is to connect a hosepipe to the cold-water tap at the kitchen sink, which can be tricky if the connector comes loose all the time, as mine used to! Outdoor tap (bib tap) kits are available from DIY stores. You will need a self-cutting valve with an integral double-check feature, a flexible hose with a protective sleeve, and a brass, outside tap with hose connector and brass wall plate.

PREPARATION

Before you start work, shut off the mains water supply. Select a suitable position for the tap; ideally, this should be within about 80 cm (32 in) of the cold mains water-supply pipe, after the rising-main stop valve, and a suitable distance from the floor — that is, high enough to get a bucket underneath!

For a unique touch, you can also buy cute decorative outdoor taps in the shape of birds and animals!

Use a small pad of wire wool to clean the supply pipe where the inside valve will be fitted. Unscrew the valve body from the clamp and then remove both the slotted screws. Position the clamp around the pipe, making sure that the profiled sealing washer is in position. Insert and tighten the screws gently to grip the pipe.

Screw the self-cutting valve into the clamp so that the cutter pierces the pipe. Adjust the valve so that it is vertical and tighten the lock nut against the clamp. Attach the flexible hose to the valve. Drill a 2.5-cm (1-in) access hole through the wall from the inside. Pass the hose through the hole. Next follow the instructions opposite for installing the outdoor tap.

SUPPLY PIPE

CLAMP

SLOTTED SCREWS

LOCK NUT

SELF-CUTTING VALVE

ANATOMY

Because the tap is connected to the main supply, a double-seal, non-return valve must be fitted between the mains pipe and the tap. This keeps contaminated water from being drawn back into the mains supply. If you intend to use a tap installation kit, then the self-cutting valve assembly also serves as the non-return valve. A flexible hose means you have no complicated pipe bends to create when running the supply through the wall.
❶ Angled bib tap and threaded nozzle ❷ Length of plastic overflow tube ❸ Drain valve ❹ Double-seal non-return valve ❺ Stop valve

WARNING

☞ Make sure there are no concealed pipes or cables in the wall before you start drilling.

1 Choose a suitable position for the wall plate on the outside wall. Hold the plate to the wall and mark each screw hole using the point of a bradawl. Using the smaller bit, drill a hole at each of the marked points, then insert wall plugs into each. Screw the plate securely to the wall.

2 Slide the compression nut and the olive on to the brass spigot end of the flexible hose, then screw it to the wall plate. Tighten it manually, then use the spanner to tighten with one turn only – do not over-tighten. Wrap a strip of PTFE tape clockwise around the thread before assembly to provide a watertight seal.

3 Attach the tap to the wall plate to complete the job. Again, wrap a short strip of PTFE tape clockwise around the thread to ensure a watertight seal.

4 To test, turn the mains supply on and open the outside tap to flush out any debris. Close the outside tap and check all the joints for signs of leakage. You can now fill up your bucket with water!

OH, STEVE, TURN OFF THE STOPCOCK BEFORE SOMETHING HAPPENS THAT WE'LL BOTH REGRET!

need

* self-cutting valve with integral double-check feature
* flexible hose with protective sleeve
* brass outdoor tap with hose connector
* brass wall plate
* bradawl
* screwdriver
* spanner
* drill and 25-mm (1-in) diameter masonry bit
* 6-mm (¼-in) diameter masonry bit
* wire wool
* all-purpose sealant
* PTFE tape

NOW THAT'S WHAT I CALL A TURN-ON!

Getting to grips with pipes

CUTTING PIPES

👉 Here's how you should deal with pipe cutting. First, buy yourself a pipe cutter. This looks a lot like a G-clamp, but has a cutting wheel and an adjustable screw with small rollers on the end. It also has a little triangular blade that pulls out to de-burr the cut edge of the pipe. This device will cut pipes at an exact ninety-degree angle every time.

❋ NO WAY, HONEY! YOU'RE NOT CUTTING THIS PIPE!

NO PIPE CUTTER?

👉 As an alternative to buying a pipe cutter, you can cut a pipe with a hacksaw. It's much harder work, but not too difficult. Wrap a strip of paper around the tube, matching up the straight edges, and attach it with a piece of masking tape. Cut through the pipe using the edge of the paper as a guide; this way the cut will be straight and at right angles to the pipe.

❶ Calculate the length of pipe needed and mark the pipe accordingly. Place the pipe in the cutter and align the circular blade with the cutting line. If the pipe is old or dirty, then clean the area to be cut using a small pad of wire wool. This will ensure that the blade makes a good cut.

need
* length of pipe to cut
* pencil
* pipe cutter

❷ Tighten the screw to hold the pipe firmly, then rotate the pipe slowly, tightening the screw a little after every revolution. The blade will cut cleanly through the metal after a few turns. Proceed slowly and do not be tempted to adjust the screw too quickly, because this may dent the pipe.

❸ The action of the pipe cutter ensures a smooth edge on the outside of the pipe but not the inside. Snap open the de-burring blade and insert it into the end of the pipe. Rotate the pipe against the tool, smoothing the rough edges and taking off all the burrs.

Pipe cutter

REPAIRING AN OUTDOOR TAP

Basic tap repairs are not difficult — all you need is a spanner and a firm grip. If the tap leaks from the spout when in the closed position, then you'll probably find that the rubber washer inside has worn out. A bib tap is a primitive beast; there's no special outer cover to remove, and the headgear is exposed and is therefore quite easy to dismantle.

❋ DON'T WORRY, I'VE SNIPPED LOTS OF PIPES BEFORE!

need
* large, adjustable spanner
* screwdriver
* new washer

1 Firmly grip the tap handle and place the jaws of the spanner around the headgear lock nut. Adjust the spanner so that it grips the nut tightly. While maintaining your grip on the handle, rotate the spanner to loosen the nut. You may have to grit your teeth a bit while you do this, but it will eventually come loose!

2 Unscrew the headgear from the tap casing. You will see a black rubber washer on a little button (or held in place by a screw) at the base of the assembly. Gently prise the washer off the button. Use a screwdriver if necessary. If the washer is held in place by a screw, unscrew it to remove the washer.

3 Replace the washer and reassemble the tap. Just to make sure that all screw joints are watertight and sealed, wrap a little PTFE tape around the threads before reassembly.

TIP
Dismantle the tap, then remove the washer. Take the old one to the shop with you to make sure the new one is the same size.

Lots more fun to be had with water in the garden

43

MENDING A HOSE

Do you have an old hosepipe? A kind friend gave her old hose to me when I moved to my new flat, and I was of course delighted to receive it. However, it soon sprang a leak, as old hoses tend to do. It is possible to attempt a makeshift repair with a puncture-repair kit or some adhesive tape, but why bodge it when you can just get a hose-repair unit like this and do the job properly? I was amazed at the range of hose gadgets and attachments that are readily available these days. A hose-repair connector is a wonderful device that can be used either to make repairs or join lengths together. Easy!

To make sure that your hose has a long and efficient life, follow the hose-care instructions on the right.

HOSE CARE

Always coil your hose neatly after use, or, better still, mount it on a reel so that it won't get tangled. Try not to leave a long hose trailing all over the garden for someone to trip over. Many hoses are green so that they are almost invisible in the grass. Make sure that your hose has no kinks in it, because these can hinder water flow. If the hose doesn't work when you try to use it, on no account look down the end to see what's wrong, you could get a jet of water right in your eye.

1 Cut out the damaged section of the hose using a Stanley knife. Unscrew both plastic ends of the connector, exposing the central part of the unit. Slip one of the ends on to each piece of hose, making sure that the thread faces the cut end. Now push the hose ends into the grips of the central unit.

2 Make sure that both ends of the hose fit snugly in the central unit, then screw on the end parts tightly. This action causes the prongs of the plastic grip to squeeze the hose, thus making a good watertight seal. Because this process doesn't involve glue, you can undo the connection at any time – perhaps to add a longer section of hose.

need
* Stanley knife
* hose-repair connector

Water the garden and pot plants during the coolest part of the day to help minimize evaporation.

EVERY GIRL APPRECIATES A NEAT HOSE!

MAINTAINING A SPRINKLER SYSTEM

44

An in-ground sprinkler system is a wonderful labour-saving device, particularly if you have a large lawn or if you're an avid gardener with vegetable patches and other areas that need regular irrigation. Check the sprinkler heads from time to time to see that they're not clogged with dirt or limescale deposits. If you spring a leak, then you'll need to dig down to the pipe and repair it. This will make you wish that the previous owner had left you the sprinkler-pipe plan.

✳ ADJUST THE UMBRELLA, SON, YOUR MOTHER'S TESTING THE SPRINKLER AGAIN!

POSITIONING A SPRINKLER

45

First, think about your dimensions. Make a scaled-down plan of the lawn, planting areas, walkways and so on. Take this along when you buy the essential components. It will be of use to you and the salesperson. Sprinkler systems are available in kit form and are easily installed. A typical kit includes all the pieces you need: sprinkler heads, an anti-syphon valve, a timer and lots of PVC pipe. Garden centres are bristling with new systems that are easy to install, so shop around. Read all the instructions thoroughly before starting work. The diagram shows a typical sprinkler system with underground pipes, sprinklers and a timer control.

OUTDOOR SOCKET   TIMER   SPRINKLER HEAD

CONTROL VALVE   VACUUM BRACKET   T-CONNECTOR   T-CONNECTOR   SPRINKLER BODY

1 Mark the pipe routes on the ground surface using string or a series of pegs.

2 Dig a narrow V-shaped trench of about 15–25 cm (6–10 in) depth, depending on the length of the sprinkler heads, along the lines.

3 Roll out the PVC pipe along the trenches, placing sprinklers on the ground at the correct positions. When all the pipes have been laid, join up the sprinklers as indicated in the instructions, then replace the soil in the trenches.

4 Now that you've done most of the hard digging, get a plumber in to complete the job (i.e. fitting the anti-syphon device, timer and connection to the mains water supply).

Simple steps to laundry heaven

PUTTING UP A WASHING LINE

46

On a warm, sunny, breezy day, there's something really satisfying about hanging your washing out to dry. Clothes dried in the sunshine have a lovely fresh smell, too. My small flat is definitely not suited to washing, so I love the summer — I can peg everything on the line and my washing is dry in no time. Better than racks of damp clothes cluttering up your living space, and much better for your house guests, too!

① Choose the position for the hook, then use your ladder to reach the area safely. Mark the hole position with chalk. Fit your drill with a big fat 12-mm (½-in) masonry bit. You need a heavy-duty plug for the heavy-duty hook; damp washing can be really heavy and you don't want the hook to come out. Put on your safety goggles and drill the hole.

② Blow into the hole to remove brick or masonry dust, then use a hammer to tap the wall plug into the hole so that the rim is flush with the wall. The wall plug should fit snugly. It's a good idea to wear your tool belt so that you can carry all your equipment with you. Screw the hook into the plug.

③ Attach a cleat to the wall at a point directly below the hook at about shoulder height. Use this to secure the washing line when it's raised to its highest position (like strings on a blind).

④ Hold the cleat up to the wall and mark the screw-hole positions. Swap the drill bit for a smaller one and drill the holes where indicated – don't forget to wear your goggles. Tap a wall plug into each hole and screw the cleat into place.

need

* ladder
* drill with a 12-mm (½-in) masonry bit
* 12-mm (½-in) wall plug
* goggles
* hammer
* small masonry bit and matching plugs
* large hook
* pulley
* cleat
* washing line
* line post

⑤ You'll need the ladder again for this. Tie the washing line to a sturdy tree if you have one; if you don't, buy a metal washing-line pole and set it in concrete just like a fence post (*see page 147*). Thread the other end of the line through the pulley and hang it from the hook. Pull the washing line taut and secure the loose end around the cleat.

PUTTING IN A CAT FLAP

If you have a cat, it's a good idea to install a cat flap so that kitty can come and go as and when she pleases. Most kits contain full instructions, cutting templates and fixings. They usually have locking mechanisms, too, so that you can keep the cat in or out when you need to. This is a basic, inexpensive model but there are lots of different ones, including those that are operated by sensors on the cat's collar. I found it easier to remove the door from the frame in order to mark and cut the hole on the workbench. You can do it with the door on the frame, but it makes it a bit more difficult to use the jigsaw.

need
* cat-flap kit
* pencil
* drill
* jigsaw with scrolling blade
* screwdriver

1 Take the door off its hinges and place it flat on your workbench. Remove the cat flap from the box, read the instructions and check that you have all the fixings. Place the cutting template in position on the lower door panel; it needs to be in the centre, at least 15 cm (6 in) from the lower edge of the door. Draw around the template. Lift up the edge of the template before removing it to check that the outline is clear.

TIP
Be careful when using the jigsaw – don't cut holes in your lovely workbench!

2 Use your drill to make pilot holes just inside both top corners of the outline. Insert the jigsaw blade in the top right-hand pilot hole and begin to cut as close to the pencil outline as you can. Proceed slowly and carefully. Remove the cut-out section and discard it.

3 The cat flap comes in two parts: the flap screws to the front of the door and the trim fits on the back with a self-adhesive strip.

4 Place the front part into the cut-out area, and screw it securely in place with the screws provided. Cover the screw heads with plastic caps. Attach the trim to the back. For a finishing touch you can paint the frame to match the door!

* SHE REALLY KNOWS HOW TO MAKE AN ENTRANCE!

Open sesame — garage-door servicing

MAINTAINING GARAGE DOORS 48

Any mechanism or device with moving parts must be well maintained and lubricated if it is to operate efficiently in the long term. Garage doors are no exception and need regular attention to keep them in shape.

MAINTENANCE

You should clean and lubricate all the moving parts of your garage doors — roller bearings, pulleys, lock mechanisms and cables — at least once a year to avoid problems and a sticky door. All you need to do is inspect every part of the mechanism and brush away any accumulated grease or dirt using a small brush. Once you've got rid of the grease and grime, put your gloves on and give everything a quick spray with an aerosol. Don't forget the lock mechanisms, because they can seize up and cause problems if neglected for a long time. Spray some lubricant into the keyhole, then work the key in and out a few times to make sure all is operating efficiently. If your doors are hinged and open outwards, then simply oil the hinges. Check for loose hinges and brackets as well and tighten them where necessary.

AND TYPES OF GARAGE DOOR

Sectional overhead doors

❋ Sectional overhead doors are usually made from metal panels that hinge together and slide on a pair of tracks inside the garage. The door retracts when opened, which is useful if space is limited and it would be inconvenient for the doors to swing outwards. Key areas to take care of on these doors are the tracks and the hinges between the door panels to ensure a smooth action.

Up-and-over doors

❋ Typical up-and-over-style doors are counterbalanced and slide on a pair of vertical tracks, one on each side of the doorway. The lower portion of the door swings outwards, then slides upwards and over into the garage. This type of door requires a certain amount of effort to open and close it, so you can see why it's important to keep all the moving parts well lubricated.

METAL PANEL   TRACK

DOOR SWINGS OUT THEN UP   TRACK

WARNING

☛ A word about fancy, electric, automatic garage-door openers. Check that these have an automatic reversing mechanism, so that if the door meets with any resistance during the closing operation, it will reverse. This means that it won't close on you or your car. If it doesn't have this feature, it is potentially dangerous.

❋ FAULTY GARAGE DOORS? ALLOW ME AND MY TRUSTY CHOPPER TO HELP YOU OUT!

need
❋ small brush
❋ gloves
❋ aerosol lubricant

GARAGE-DOOR MECHANISM

☞ Before installation can take place, a solid wood frame must be fitted securely around the doorway to give adequate clearance at the sides and the top and to provide firm attachment points for the mechanism. Some companies will include a frame with the door, and this will be included in the overall measurement. Automatic door opening mechanisms can be fitted to most sectional or up-and-over garage doors. These devices are electrically operated and make your life so much easier – no more hauling a heavy door up and down. Usually the door is opened remotely from inside or out using a handheld control. If you need to replace a garage door or opening mechanism, then this will be a job for a professional – maintenance is the easy part.

SAFETY CABLE

STUD PULLEY

DOOR LOCK

LOCK BAR

CABLE ANCHOR

THAWING FROZEN PIPES

49

Winter brings cold weather, and — if you're unlucky — frozen pipes. Prevention is better than cure so try to insulate vulnerable pipes, like those that run through lofts, basements or under floors. If the tank won't fill or a tap refuses to work, this is a sure sign that water has frozen in one of the supply pipes. Outdoor taps are prime targets for winter freeze-ups. Locate the problematic pipe and direct hot air from a hairdryer over the affected part. Copper pipes conduct heat quickly and the ice plug inside the pipe will melt, resulting in normal water flow. Leave the tap open so that you know when the problem has been solved.

✻ GREAT JOB ON THE DOORS, HONEY! HOW D'YA WORK THIS ROUND THING?

Water, water, everywhere...how to deal with floods and blockages

Or you could just call the fire brigade and watch them do it instead!

PUMPING OUT A BASEMENT

50

Crisis! You have a flood in your basement. If the flood was caused by a burst pipe, turn off the water supply by turning off the main stop valve. Put on your wellies and rubber gloves and salvage anything of value. Think about how such an event can be avoided in the future: make sure that all pipes that run under floorboards, through basements or in loft areas are properly insulated. I used to live in a house where the basement would fill with water from time to time — something to do with the water table, I was told. This kind of periodic water-level rise is a nuisance. If you are unfortunate enough to have a problem like this on your hands, hire a submersible pump and hose. The hire-shop staff will show you how to use the equipment safely and efficiently. The pump is placed under the water and pumps it out through the hose. You must make sure that the end of the pipe is near a main drain so that it runs away safely. When all the water has been pumped away, you can hire a big hot-air blower to dry the area out.

need
* wellingtons
* rubber gloves
* submersible pump and hose
* hot-air blower

Submersible pump and hose

THIS YEAR'S ABSOLUTE MUST HAVES!

AND

TACKLING DAMPNESS

Dampness in basements may not be caused by flooding. Because the basement is underground, or partially underground, excessive condensation can form on the walls because they are colder than the air inside the basement. This kind of dampness can be treated by applying a specially formulated sealant to the walls and floors to create a barrier. To determine whether the dampness is seeping in/up from the surrounding ground or is the result of condensation, try a few elimination processes. Make sure that the basement is well ventilated and hire/buy a dehumidifier unit. Still damp? Check that all rainwater drainage systems are clear and functioning effectively; there might be a blocked downpipe overflowing next to the basement. Patios might have settled and dropped a little, directing water towards the house and basement. A nearby tree might be interfering with your foundations. If the source isn't obvious, call in the experts.

UNBLOCKING MAIN DRAINS

Blocked drains are pretty unpleasant, but sometimes you just have to grit your teeth and get on with the task.

TAKE THE PLUNGE

If you have a blockage in a toilet that a plunger won't solve, try using a WC auger, a shorter version of a drain auger. If that doesn't work, the blockage could be in a branch drain below the affected toilet or in the main drain. For this, you'll need drain rods. Lift the manhole cover on the drain run from the soil stack (it will be very heavy). If the chamber is full, remove the plug from the rodding eye at the 'downstream' end of the chamber, screw the rods together and pass them through to clear the blockage. Always turn the rods clockwise, otherwise they may come unscrewed. If the chamber is empty, rod towards the soil stack. If the blockage is in the stack, place a bucket beneath the cleaning eye, unscrew the eye and insert a drain auger. Turn the handle to clear the blockage. Flush with fresh water and disinfect everything.

need
- rubber gloves
- drain rods
- drain-rod attachments
- disinfectant

Plunger head

Scraper head

Corkscrew head

Drain-rod attachments

These scary-looking torture instruments are drain-rod attachments. You can hire a set to deal with the most stubborn of blockages (*see also page 20*). Just put your rubber gloves on, push the rods with desired attachment into the drain, then push and pull until the blockage clears.

WE MAY LOOK STIFF, BUT WE CAN BEND TO FIT ANYWHERE!

※ I ALWAYS MOISTURIZE AFTER A LONG, HARD SESSION WITH MY FLEXIBLE RODS!

Drain rods

These are flexible rods that join together, and they come with a selection of fittings to attach to the end – plungers, corkscrews and scrapers (*see above*).

TIP
If all else fails, call in the pros.

Making a bird table 52

Now that you've completed all that exterior maintenance, why not get creative and make a pretty bird table to add a nice finishing touch to the garden? As we all know, birds have a hard time finding enough food during the winter months, so I'm sure they'll be very pleased to have a helping hand. Make sure that you place the bird table in a quiet spot so the birds will not be disturbed or frightened away by passers by. It's also good to place the bird table near a window so that you can watch the birds. Birds like bread, seeds and nuts, and be sure to put a dish of fresh water out for them, too — they may drink it or even bathe in it!

need

* pencil and tracing paper
* pine board or old hardwood shelving
* 32-mm x 12-mm (1¼-in x ½-in) wooden battens
* piece of plywood for the base
* wooden fence post
* metal fence-post spike
* sledgehammer
* four small brass right-angle brackets plus screws
* wooden plant markers
* feather-edge fence boards
* jigsaw
* abrasive paper
* saw
* hammer
* 25-mm (1-in) nails
* screwdriver
* household scissors
* masking tape
* exterior gloss paint
* paintbrush
* artist's paintbrush
* wood glue

1 To begin, trace the templates (*see page 182*), then redraw each at full size. You will need a front, a back and two sides. Cut out the paper templates and draw the outlines on the pine board. Use a jigsaw to cut out the shapes, then smooth off any rough edges using abrasive paper.

2 Cut four 25-cm (10-in)-long wooden battens. These will be used to strengthen the walls of the bird table where they meet at each corner. Use wood glue to attach the battens to the side pieces.

3 Press firmly into position to expel any excess glue, which should be wiped away before it dries. When the glue is dry, nail the battens securely in place.

4 You now need to attach four battens in place across the base of the archways on all four sides to support the shape (and to keep the bird food from falling out). At the front and back, cut, glue and nail battens to fit exactly across the arch.

5 For the sides, attach the battens in the same way, but make them a little longer at each end to accommodate the width of the battens on the front and back. When the sides are nailed together, the battens form a little wall all around. Construct the house as shown in the diagram on page 182. Don't forget the stabilizing batten at the apex.

✳ HIGH-RISE LIVING? IT'S FOR THE BIRDS!

6 Use your scissors to cut the wooden plant markers in half; you will need about twenty halves. Take two spare pieces of batten and attach the ends of each half-marker to the battens with pieces of masking tape. Paint half the markers pink and half of them blue on both sides.

7 Cut a piece of plywood to fit the base, then glue and nail it in place. Paint the bird table inside and out. When the paint is dry, use wood glue to stick the painted markers to the inside of the perimeter wall down both sides, just like a picket fence.

8 Cut six pieces of fence board, about 10 cm (4 in) longer than the measurement across the roof from front to back. Paint six pieces pink and two blue. Nail the pieces in place on the roof, starting at the lower eaves and working up towards the apex, overlapping as you go. The boards should protrude by about 5 cm (2 in) at the front and back and along the eaves.

TIP
I've used some old hardwood shelves to make the sides of the bird table here, but pine board is just as good. Prime and paint it with exterior-quality paint to protect it.

9 To mount the bird table, first paint the fence post, then drive the metal fence-post spike into the ground. Place the fence post in the spike: you may have to help it a little with the sledgehammer (*see page 146, 'Installing a panel fence'*). Attach it to the underside of the table using brass screws and right-angle brackets.

GETTING GROUNDED

Get your back garden back into great shape with lovely lawns, perfect patios, delightful decking and so much more...

Making the garden lovely

LET'S START at ground level, shall we? If you're lucky enough to have inherited a beautiful garden, then you should just feel very pleased with yourself, sit somewhere comfortable and relax. But if, as in my case, your garden is a bit of a jungle (admittedly, mine got like that through sheer neglect — well, I was working on my flat!), one of the first things you'll need to do in the garden is clear up.

CLEANING AND PAINTING A CONCRETE FLOOR

Concrete surfaces in garden areas and concrete floors in garages and basements tend to be magnets for dirt and grime. The textured surface captures dirt and oily stains and eventually looks rather worn. It might even become dangerous to walk on, especially in wet weather. Give the floor a really good clean, then apply a coat or two of heavy-duty floor paint to create an attractive anti-slip surface (most paints of this type contain anti-slip agents). You can choose a neutral colour or go for a complete change. Pink concrete — just imagine!

TIP
Remove rust stains from concrete using bleach and a small, stiff brush.

1 Before using detergents or water, brush away surface debris and organic matter using a stiff brush. If there are any stubborn oil stains to remove, use a specially formulated cleaner worked undiluted into the stain with a small brush. Leave for the length of time specified by the manufacturer, then rinse with a solution of four parts water to one part cleaner, again applied with a stiff brush.

2 If the concrete is not stained but simply grubby with ingrained dirt, a pressure washer should do the trick. Put on your wellingtons, connect the washer to a tap with a hosepipe and away you go.

3 The water jet dislodges stubborn dirt, leaving shiny, clean concrete; the difference in colour is amazing. Allow to dry before applying any paint or sealer.

4 If the surface of the clean concrete is dusty or porous, apply a coat of sealer – this will help the top coat of paint go further. Decant the sealer into a shallow paint tray placed on the floor near your feet. Use a roller with an extending handle to save your back. When the sealer is dry, apply a coat or two of floor paint in the colour of your choice, using a roller as before.

need
- stiff brush
- small hand brush
- cleaning product for driveways/patios
- bucket
- low-pressure washer
- hosepipe
- rubber gloves
- wellingtons
- long-handled roller
- paint tray
- heavy-duty floor paint
- sealer (optional)

BUSH CLEARING AND TRIMMING

54

When the time for jungle clearance arrives, wear wellingtons, put on your gloves and resign yourself to hard work. It is best to do this in the autumn when plants are dying back. Work from the top downwards: first, prune and trim trees, bushes and large shrubs, then attack lower-growing plants. After that, get down in the dirt, turning over the topsoil along borders and removing any weeds and undesirables as you go. Last but not least, mow the grass!

1 Secateurs are usually sufficient for general low, light undergrowth and bush clearance, but when you're faced with high or thick branches, a long-handled lopper is what you need. Simply snip off the offending branches.

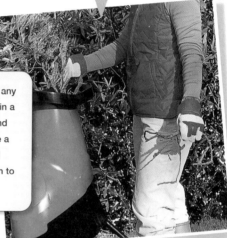

2 Collect all the pruned and trimmed branches and any other woody organic matter, and set up your shredder in a level position. Feed the trimmings into the shredder and let it do all the hard work for you! Don't forget to place a large bag underneath the outlet to catch the shredded pieces. The resulting chippings make a fabulous mulch to use along the borders of garden pathways.

YOU WILL NOT BELIEVE WHAT I'VE JUST SEEN!

need

* gloves
* wellingtons
* mower
* secateurs
* lopper
* shredder
* leaf rake
* hand trowel and fork
* large bags to collect debris

SAVE LEAVES FOR THE COMPOST!

WARNING

☞ You will probably need to use an outdoor extension lead for the shredder, so remember to use a circuit breaker.

PRUNING AND LOPPING

Keeping small trees in shape is simple, and it will help them to stay healthy. All you need is a pruning saw, a pruning knife and a little spare time.

☞ Using a pruning saw, make a cut about halfway through the branch on the underside, approximately 25 cm (10 in) from the trunk.
☞ Now make a second cut close to the first, from the top downwards, again about halfway through the branch.
☞ The branch will break free quite easily.
☞ Saw off the remaining stump so that it lies flush with the main trunk or branch. Trim off any leaves from cut branches and save them for the compost.

Keeping the lawn in tip-top condition

LAWN MAINTENANCE 55

Lawns don't just look after themselves; they need lots of tender loving care if you want them to stay green and pleasant. Mowing is probably the first thing that comes to mind, but don't mow every week come what may; you need only trim the grass when it needs it. A scalped lawn will quickly go brown in hot weather. As a general rule of thumb, remove about 2 cm (¾ in) each time. I take the quick back-and-sides approach, but you could go for stripes or checkered patterns if you really have a lot of time on your hands.

If neighbours' animals have got into the habit of using your lovely lawn at their convenience, make sure that your fences and gates are secure and that there are no big gaps through which your unwelcome visitors can squeeze. If the problem persists, buy a chemical deterrent from a garden centre. These products are not harmful, but they have odours that are unpleasant to the relevant animals.

TIP

Remember, earthworms are great! Their burrows run deep into the ground, creating good drainage channels and aerating the soil.

2 Press the fork down firmly with the sole of your foot and wiggle it back and forth a little to create holes in the soil – this will encourage drainage and air flow in the lawn. Do this at intervals of about 30 cm (12 in). You can also buy aerating machines for this.

1 Aerate the lawn from time to time using a garden fork. Put on your boots and place the tines of the fork on the surface of the ground.

3 Lawns look absolutely fabulous if the edges are well manicured. In order to achieve this level of splendour, use an edging tool. Its sharp, semi-circular blade cuts through untidy edges beautifully, leaving a nice, neat shape. You can also use it to make lovely circles round trees or shrubs, or sweeping curves round larger areas.

WARNING

☞ When using any electrical appliance outdoors, it is of the utmost importance that you take all the necessary precautions to ensure your own safety and that of others. If you do not have a professionally installed, waterproof, external electric socket, use a heavy-duty extension lead, suitable for outdoor use, in conjunction with a Residual Current Device (RCD). RCDs automatically 'trip' and cut off the current if there is a power overload. Be extremely careful when running devices with extension leads (for example, lawn mowers or strimmers); always drape the lead over your shoulder and mow forwards with the lead trailing behind you, out of harm's way. Never mow while walking backwards – you might accidentally cut the lead.

TIP

Do you like daisies? I do. Weeds are a matter of preference. Decide what you want and what you don't want, and act accordingly. Get a spot weedkiller spray to deal with scattered patches of weeds without damaging the grass.

LAYING TURF

Turf isn't that expensive when you consider that it gives you a new lawn almost instantaneously. Buy your turf from a reliable source, and get it fresh. Be very wary of turf that looks as if it's been lying around on a pallet for a while; it might be yellow or brown inside the roll and will be useless. Turf is sold by the square metre or yard, so calculate the area that you want to cover and divide it by the unit area.

1 The first thing you need to do is remove the existing turf. Use a spade to cut under the grass to remove the top layer. Make sure that the soil is relatively free of debris, stones, weeds and old turf. Rake over the entire area to make a flat surface in preparation for the new turf.

2 Begin by laying strips of turf around the outside edge of the intended lawn; narrow pieces at the edge can dry out and perish. Then lay a row of turf along the longest, straightest line you can find.

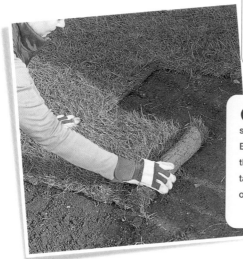

3 Lay the turf in a bricklaying pattern, so the seams are staggered from one row to the next. Butt and push the ends together, but don't stretch the turf. You can use a long wooden board to tamp the turf down after laying. Use an edging tool or a sharp knife to cut round obstacles or curves.

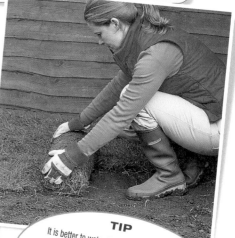

TIP
It is better to water thoroughly and infrequently, rather than giving your lawn a light sprinkle every few days. Water in the early morning and in calm weather to reduce evaporation.

AFTERCARE

☞ Now that the turf is laid, you must water, water, water! New turf needs a good soaking and regular twice-daily watering in hot, dry weather. Don't mow the new lawn until it is well rooted to the subsoil, and then just give it a trim. Never cut off more than one-third of the grass's length. Resist the temptation to walk on your fabulous new lawn for at least a couple of weeks, allowing it to root down properly.

❋ DRINK UP, BRAD, WE'VE GOT TO KEEP THIS TURF WELL WATERED!

❋ FINE, HONEY – AS LONG AS I DON'T HAVE TO SIT ON THE DAMP PATCH!

Making the most of your waste

MAKING A COMPOST BIN

56

Why not make your own compost? It's a great way to use vegetable waste such as peelings and trimmings; it's also ideal for grass clippings and fallen leaves. When you've finished your bush clearing and trimming (*see page 111*), you can save all the cut leaves for the compost bin instead of throwing them away (but don't include any branches). You can use your homemade compost for potting and general soil improvement in the garden.

need

* **lengths of 150-mm x 25-mm (6-in x 1-in) timber board**
* **50-mm x 50-mm (2-in x 2-in) softwood battens**
* **50-mm x 25-mm (2-in x 1-in) softwood battens**
* **sheet of plywood**
* **screws**
* **tenon saw**
* **hammer**
* **jigsaw**
* **drill with twist bit and 25-mm (1-in) flat bit**
* **screwdriver**

1 To construct the sides, cut two corner supports to size (*see Dimensions box opposite*) and then lay them parallel to each other about 81 cm (32 in) apart. Lay seven lengths of board across them, edge to edge.

2 Screw each board end to the supports. Make another side in the same way. Using the flat bit, drill a few holes near the centre of the lower board on each side. This will allow air to circulate.

3 Create the back by screwing seven boards to the inside of the corner supports of each side. Use two screws at the ends of each board to form a sturdy U-shaped framework. Turn the assembly on each side in turn to attach the tracks.

4 Screw a pair of track strips to the inside front edge of each side panel. Allow a space between each pair of track strips a little wider than the thickness of the boards. Screw the strips in place to form channels for the removable front boards.

5 Slot the remaining seven boards into the hatch tracks at the front of the compost bin. Don't attach them to each other; they can remain loose for easy removal when the compost needs turning or you want to take some out for use. To do this, remove a few of the top boards, then raise the lower ones enough to get your shovel in.

6 For the lid, construct a simple butt-jointed frame from 50-mm x 25-mm (2-in x 1-in) battens to fit the top of the compost bin. Screw the corners together and cut a piece of plywood to fit the top. Nail the plywood to the frame, and then cover the lid with roofing felt or plastic tarpaulin to make it waterproof.

MAKING YOUR OWN COMPOST

Save vegetable matter from the kitchen and clippings, leaves and soft vegetation waste from the garden. Pile it into the compost bin until you have a layer about 15 cm (6 in) deep. Add a layer of compost activator, which you can buy from any garden centre. This speeds up the decomposition of the vegetable matter. A thin layer of soil can also help at this stage; it keeps the decomposing matter warm and may add a few more good things, like worms. Keep layering like this to fill the bin. Turn the mass over after a month, then wait. In a few months you'll have lots of lovely compost at the bottom of the bin.

TIP
Don't include woody branches, tough roots, diseased plant material or perennial weeds in the composting mixture.

COVERED PLYWOOD

BACK BOARDS

LID BATTEN

CORNER SUPPORTS

FRONT TRACK

FIXING PEGS

SIDE BOARDS

AIR HOLES

Dimensions

Sides and back
Twenty-one 90 cm (36-in) lengths of 150-mm x 25-mm (6-in x 1-in) board
Front hatch
Seven 90 cm (36-in) lengths of 150-mm x 25-mm (6-in x 1-in) board
Corner supports
Two 107-cm (42-in) lengths of 50-mm x 50-mm (2-in x 2-in) batten
Front hatch track
Four 107-cm (42-in) lengths of 50-mm x 25-mm (2-in x 1-in) batten

A RECYCLING STATION

Most household waste can be recycled: paper, glass, plastics, cans and so on. You can do your bit to help the environment by setting aside an area in the garden for use as a recycling station. It doesn't have to be fancy – it can be a simple row of sturdy hooks along a sheltered and unobtrusive bit of garden wall. Simply hang up bags for each recyclable material: one for paper, one for cans, one for glass bottles and so on. When the bags are full, take them to the nearest recycling facility. I have an old chest in my garden in which I keep a few small plastic storage boxes. I just lift up the lid and throw my bits and pieces into the appropriate box. Easy!

Getting down to earth
LEVELLING GROUND 58

If you're considering a dry-laid (mortarless) paved or brick patio, or making a base for a small shed, this section is essential reading. The site must be absolutely level and well compacted before you begin — cheat at this stage and you'll be disappointed with the results. The advantage of dry-laid paving is that you don't have to build in a drainage slope. Rainwater will simply drain through the gaps between the pavers or bricks. If a fully mortared paved area is laid perfectly flat, water will gather in pools and you'll have a wet patio. Also, consider location: for sunbathing, your patio should face south or west, but if you're planning alfresco dinner parties, choose a shady spot (near the kitchen).

SITE PREPARATION

☞ Mark out the site using a bricklayer's line and pegs. Measure the area and place a peg at each corner (if your area is square or rectangular), and tie lengths of line tightly between the pegs. Check that the corners are at right angles. You don't need to set up formwork, or edging, for a dry-laid project as you would for a concrete surface, but it's a good idea. Nail long planks to wooden pegs and drive them into the ground along the perimeter of the site. The forms make a good containing frame for compacting and provide a straight edge when it's time to lay the slabs or pavers. You will then need to remove the topsoil to accommodate the depth of the pavers or bricks, and add gravel and sand layers so the top of the patio will be level with the surrounding ground.

① Cut the wooden battens into lots of 25-cm (10-in) lengths. Using a Stanley knife, whittle one end of each length to a point. These pegs act as depth guides when you're applying the layers and tamping down.

② From the top of each peg, mark the depth of the slab/brick, sand and ballast layers. The sand and ballast layers should each be about 2.5–5 cm (1–2 in) thick when compacted. To keep your clothing clean, kneel on landscaping material. If the ground is very wet, use a plastic rubbish bag because the landscaping material will allow moisture through.

③ Use a hammer to drive the marker peg into the excavated earth. The top of each peg should be at ground level. Place markers at regular intervals around the perimeter of the site, and at points across the area, too (if your patio is quite small then you can probably do without these).

④ Lay the long levelling/tamping board across the top of the marker pegs, and lay the spirit level on top. Check that all the pegs are level with each other around the edge and across the entire site. If any of the pegs are standing too high, simply drive them into the earth a little further and check the level again. It is very important that these markers are accurate.

5 Now for the labour-intensive part – tamping! Using the levelling/tamping board, flatten and compact the excavated earth. Lay the board horizontally and lift and drop it repeatedly on to the earth. You can stand up and use the end of the board if your back isn't up to it. The general idea is to compact the earth as solidly as possible, making a firm base for the ballast and sand layers.

* IF I CAN'T SKATE ON IT, IT AIN'T LEVEL!

6 The fully compacted earth should be at the level indicated on your marker pegs. Use the levelling/tamping board and the spirit level to check your progress.

7 If your tamping has been particularly effective, you may have to put some of the excavated earth back in to bring the level up to the mark. This stage is quite important, because a badly compacted base may cause subsidence later on. One final levelling, then proceed to the next sections.

WARNING

☞ The surface of any paved area near your house must be at least 15 cm (6 in) below the damp-proof course in the wall. If the surface is above this, moisture will seep into your home, causing serious problems!

need

* long planks to make forms (optional, but a good idea)
* hammer
* nails
* shovel
* gravel
* landscaping material
* spirit level
* sand
* Stanley knife
* 25-mm x 25-mm (1-in x 1-in) wooden battens for layer markers
* levelling/tamping board (could be any length of wood)
* bricklayer's line and pegs

Walk this way

LAYING A PAVED PATIO

Paving slabs are the simplest option for patios. The ones I've used here are the very basic man-made ones, readily available and inexpensive if you're on a tight budget. If you want natural materials, pretty colours and/or elaborate shapes, then you're going to pay more. Spend a bit of time at a DIY store writing down prices, sizes and types of slab or paving stone, then work out how much it's going to cost before you start. Many stores sell decorative paving in kit form, so if you feel adventurous you could design something more stylish.

Estimating the quantities

Use a calculator if your arithmetic isn't up to scratch! To calculate roughly how many slabs you will need, measure the length and width of your site, then divide each measurement by the measurement of the slab. Multiply the two results together to get the number of slabs needed. Alternatively, multiply the length of the site by the width to obtain the area in square metres or square yards, then calculate the number of slabs using the quick guide below.

45-cm x 45-cm slabs: 5 per square metre (18-in x 18-in slabs: 4 per square yard)

60-cm x 60-cm slabs: 2.75 per square metre (24-in x 24-in: 2.25 per square yard)

Buy a few spares in case you need to cut some to fit.

1 Have your bags of ballast handy. Empty them over the compacted earth. Use the levelling board to spread the ballast out (you could use a rake if preferred).

2 Don't empty all the bags in one big pile in the middle if you're working over a large area; small piles dotted all over are better! When all the ballast is in place, begin to tamp down using the levelling board. This can be hard work, but it is worth doing well. Remember to check the levels as you go, using the spirit level and the guide markers.

3 Cut a piece of landscaping material to fit your area. You can use several overlapped pieces if necessary. Landscaping material is a wonderful invention; it allows water to pass through to the earth beneath, but does not allow weeds or other organic material to push upwards, ruining your lovely patio.

4 Now for the sand layer. Follow the same procedure as for the ballast, emptying the bags in turn and raking or spreading it out to cover the whole area to a uniform depth. Tamp the sand down firmly using the levelling board once again, checking with the guide markers as you go. Add more sand to any thin areas if necessary.

5 It's time to lay the first course of paving slabs! Begin by laying a slab in one corner, squaring one corner of the slab up against the corner of a form. Lay one complete row in this way using the form as a straightedge. You can also indicate straight lines with a bricklayer's line and pegs, then use the strings as your guide. If your patio is small, then you can space the slabs by eye, but use thin, wooden battens to create uniform spaces between the slabs if you have a large area to cover. Check each slab using the spirit level as you go.

6 Continue to lay rows of whole slabs until the area is covered. If you have to work round awkward shapes, leave the slab-cutting until the end. Finally, check that all the slabs are level with each other using the levelling board and spirit level, and make any adjustments with the rubber mallet. Make sure that you check the levels across the patio diagonally in both directions, too.

CUTTING SLABS

☛ If it's possible to plan your patio so that you can avoid cutting paving slabs, do so — save yourself some time and effort! However, if your patio area does not allow this, you'll have to cut. You will need a brick bolster and a club hammer, a small wooden block and safety goggles.

TIP
Most DIY stores sell decorative paving – circles, semi-circles or shaped slabs, for example – in kit form. If you're feeling creative, you could design something more distinctive than a basic grid.

7 Finally, brush in dry sand to pack the gaps between the paving slabs, and wet thoroughly with a hosepipe. This is the advantage of mortarless paving: any rainwater will drain away easily through the gaps, so you won't have puddles.

1 First of all, put on your safety goggles. Mark the cutting line across the paving slab with some chalk. Using the brick bolster and hammer, make a groove along the chalk line. Score the paving slab in this way on both sides and at the edges as well.

2 Place the paving slab on a bed of sand, and place the wooden block at one end of the groove. Use the club hammer to strike the wooden block while you move it along the groove. Eventually, the paving slab will break.

need

* enough slabs to cover the area, plus a few spares
* ballast
* landscaping material
* bricklayer's sand
* shovel and rake
* brick bolster
* club hammer and rubber mallet
* brush
* bricklayer's line and pegs
* spacers (optional)
* levelling board
* spirit level

Make a bricktastic patio

LAYING A BRICK PATIO

61

Paving bricks, or pavers, make extremely attractive patio surfaces. They are much smaller than paving slabs, so there is greater scope for creativity when planning the area. They can be laid in numerous configurations or 'bonds' — forty-five- or ninety-degree herringbone, groups of two, interlocked end-to-end...whatever pattern takes your fancy (*see box below for some suggestions*). However, it is very important to remember that because bricks are smaller than slabs, they will need some kind of permanent edging at the perimeter to keep them from spreading out of shape. You can use decorative edgings or bricks laid end-to-end for this purpose.

1 Prepare the site for the ballast layer. Use a rake or the levelling board to spread out each load of ballast to cover the area completely. Tamp thoroughly using the levelling board, checking at intervals using the marker pegs as a guide.

BRICK PATTERNS

Because bricks are smaller than paving slabs, the creative scope for layout is greater. Choose simple basketweave or herringbone styles like these or more elaborate styles. Remember, the more complicated the pattern, the more likely you are to have awkward-shaped gaps to fill when the design is complete!

STAGGERED BASKETWEAVE

HERRINGBONE BOND

2 Make sure that all the material is well compacted and check it using a board and spirit level. If there are any thin areas, add some more ballast and retamp. When you are satisfied, move on to the next step. Do not be tempted to rush the preparation stages, as it is important to create a perfectly level and solid base for your patio to sit on.

3 Cut a single piece of landscaping material to fit the patio area if possible, or use smaller overlapping pieces.

Estimating the quantities

To calculate approximately how many bricks you'll need, measure the length and width of your site and the length and width of a brick. Divide one side of the area by the largest brick measurement, and the other side by the shortest brick measurement. Multiply the two results to get the number of bricks needed. Or multiply both site measurements to get the area in square metres or square yards, then calculate the number of bricks needed using this quick guide: 200-mm x 100-mm bricks: 50 bricks per square metre (7¾-in x 4-in bricks: 42 bricks per square yard).

4 Now for the sand layer. Empty the bags in turn over the patio area, and use a rake or board to spread the sand evenly. Then tamp the sand to a uniform depth across the patio, using the marker pegs as a guide. Check the level using the spirit level and board, and retamp if necessary to flatten out any bumps. Add extra sand to thin areas.

TIP

Each paver has a chamfered edge on one side so that you'll know which way is up, and they have moulded spacers along each edge, so you don't have to worry about that either!

5 Use the diagrams provided as guides or design a pattern of your own. This is quite a speedy procedure: it won't take very long to lay the whole area. I used a basic ninety-degree herringbone pattern.

6 Place a row of bricks end-to-end around the patio perimeter, or use decorative edging stones. By now you should have decided which pattern you'd like to use, so begin by laying whole bricks in an orderly sequence.

7 Finally, fill in all the remaining spaces with half-bricks or diagonally cut bricks (see 'Cutting Brick' box below for a simple guide). When all the bricks are down, sweep dry sand over the entire surface, packing it into all the spaces. Wet the area thoroughly using a hosepipe.

CUTTING BRICKS IS A GREAT STRESS RELIEVER – PRETEND IT'S YOUR EX!

need

* enough pavers to cover area, plus spares for cutting
* ballast
* landscaping material
* bricklayer's sand
* shovel
* rake
* brick bolster
* club hammer
* brush
* levelling board
* spirit level
* rubber mallet

CUTTING BRICK

62

☞ You will need a brick bolster, a club hammer, gloves and safety goggles. Lay the brick on a flat surface and place the bolster blade on the halfway point (you could mark it with chalk first if you like). Strike the bolster firmly along the line to score it, then strike along the line a few more times: the brick should break in half cleanly. Have a few spares handy in case you need to practise a bit.

121

Up the garden path
LAYING A BRICK PATH

63

Brick pavers are great for building paths. Because the units are small, you can create different patterns — ideal for a simple straight path, and even more suitable for a curved one. All you have to do is ease the pattern as you progress along the path to fit the curved shape.

need

* bricks for path and edges, plus spares
* ballast
* landscaping material
* sharp sand
* shovel
* rake
* brick bolster
* brush
* club hammer
* levelling board
* board to kneel on
* spirit level
* rubber mallet
* dry sand
* small pebbles

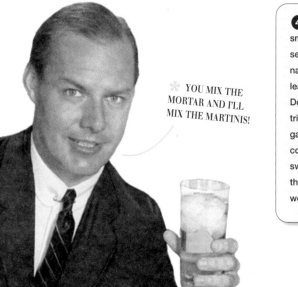

* YOU MIX THE MORTAR AND I'LL MIX THE MARTINIS!

1 Mark out a straight pathway with a bricklayer's line and pegs or long board, then excavate and compact the site between the markers.

2 Lay a row of bricks end-to-end along both sides of the path to contain the main pathway pavers, then lay the ballast, landscaping material and sand layers, compacting and levelling each layer as you progress. If the pathway is curved, use a hosepipe laid out on the ground as a guide and drive in markers to follow the shape.

3 Using a board to kneel on, lay the bricks along the intended pathway in the bonding pattern of your choice. I used a forty-five-degree herringbone pattern. If there are bends or curves in the pathway, then simply ease the brick pattern around it.

4 To complete the path, fill in the small gaps on each side. This may seem like a daunting task – it is in the nature of a herringbone pattern to leave lots of little triangular spaces. Don't panic, there's no need to cut triangular pieces of brick to fit: fill the gaps will small pebbles, gravel or coloured glass chippings. Finally, sweep dry sand over the top to fill the gaps between the bricks, then wet thoroughly using a hosepipe.

122

LAYING A GRAVEL OR BARK PATH

If your garden is a little lumpy and bumpy and you really don't relish the thought of all that excavation and levelling, then what you need is a nice gravel or mulch pathway. Gravel and mulch are relatively inexpensive and look attractive as pathway materials. The soft top layer of the pathway will mask any imperfections on the ground perfectly, so there's no need to work hard with the spirit level.

need

* bricks for edges
* ballast
* landscaping material
* sand
* shovel
* gravel or chipped bark
* rake

1 Mark the path with a bricklayer's line and pegs or long boards if it is straight. If you want a curved path, use a hosepipe as a guide and drive pegs in to follow the shape. Use an edging tool to cut along the marked edge to remove the turf if you need to.

2 Excavate and compact the site between the markers. Lay a row of bricks end-to-end along both sides of the path to contain the gravel or bark, then lay the ballast, landscaping materials and sand.

3 Empty the bags of gravel or bark in the area between the brick edges. Spread out evenly over the pathway using a rake or levelling board. The main advantage of using gravel or bark is that it can cover a multitude of sins at ground level. Any small-sized stone chippings would be a suitable alternative to using gravel here.

4 When all the gravel or bark is in place, tamp it down well using a board cut to the exact width of the path. Start at one end and work to the other, levelling out any really big bumps that you discover on the way. Keep a spare bag in the shed in case you need to replenish the path later.

AND

SITING A PATHWAY

Pathways with soft or hard surfaces get you from A to B in all weather without muddying your feet or wearing a nasty bald trail across the lawn you've worked so hard to maintain. If you have a new garden and need to decide on the best position for a pathway, wait a while and see where people walk most frequently, then put the path there. It's a waste of time and energy laying a path down one side of the garden only to find that it's easier to walk across the middle – people will always take the shortcut. Laying a walkway is simple – a sand and ballast base, along with a landscaping material layer to prevent weed growth, is all you need. Then choose your favourite topping for the path – bricks, gravel, bark, whatever you like.

The path to happiness

MAINTAINING A GARDEN PATH

Maintaining the pathway you have created is a pretty important task, and not just for aesthetic reasons. Safety is also a major concern, especially if the pathway is used frequently. It is open to the elements all year round, and snow, rain and the sun's heat all cause damage to sub-layers and sand infills, giving rise to cracks and low spots. These can make the path dangerous to walk on especially for children and the elderly. If your garden has an old pathway, regular maintenance is even more important; there is probably no weedproof layer underneath.

need

* old kitchen knife or scraper
* crowbar
* bricklayer's sand
* brush
* levelling board
* spirit level
* pressure washer
* gloves
* scrubbing brush
* weedkiller spray

1 Get rid of weeds and unwanted organic growth between the bricks or slabs and along the edges. Pull out the roots ruthlessly – some weeds are seemingly indestructible. Show no mercy! Slide the blade of an old kitchen knife or a scraper between the stones to hook out any stray pieces. Use the blade to scrape off moss, too.

2 Check that all the bricks or slabs are still level. Over time there may be a little subsidence in the sub-layers, causing the surface to rise or sink. Sudden dips in the surface can cause unsuspecting pathway users to trip or fall. Lift uneven slabs or bricks using a crowbar and repack with sand, tamping down well, then reset the brick or slab. Use a board and spirit level to check that the relaid slabs or bricks are level with their neighbours.

3 Now that the path is weeded and level, use a stiff scrubbing brush to get rid of dirt, stains, algae or slippery organic material that may have accumulated on the surface. This is a problem that occurs mainly on bricks and paving slabs, and can be very dangerous if you happen to be walking along in wet weather. If you have a pressure washer, use it! It really is the best thing for getting rid of unwanted surface gunk because it just blasts through dirt!

ANY EXCUSE TO PLAY WITH YOUR PRESSURE WASHER!

TIP
If you are replacing old brick pavers, soak the new bricks in a bucket of muddy water to give them an aged appearance.

4 If you have a persistent weed problem, then you may have to resort to chemicals in the form of weedkiller spray. The spray action means that you can direct the jet of chemical exactly where you want it, right at the weeds. These products can be used on lawns, too, because the jet can be aimed to avoid the surrounding grass. To finish, sweep dry sand over the pathway to fill any gaps between the stones.

DEALING WITH TREE ROOTS

66

Despite their beauty throughout the seasons, trees can be the cause of big problems, such as subsidence or its opposite, heave. If you have mature trees growing too near your home, they could cause structural damage. The answer might be to remove the tree completely (*see box opposite*) or chop it back. Consider the positioning of new trees carefully. When buying saplings, ask how big they are likely to be when mature and the estimated root-spread area. Plant saplings about two-thirds of the distance of the expected mature height away from any major building or shed. Better safe than sorry!

Save chopped logs of tree trunks for firewood.

ROOT PROBLEMS

SUBSIDENCE Subsidence, eventually resulting in cracks in the structure of your home, is often caused by mature trees growing too close by. The roots can draw too much moisture from the soil, causing the earth near the house to subside. This causes damage to the house foundations, leading to serious cracks.

HEAVE This is the opposite of subsidence. When a tree is removed carelessly, the surrounding ground will absorb too much moisture, causing the earth to swell. This will cause displacement and damage to the foundations. Thus it is very important not to chop down trees close to your home before getting advice from a professional.

FELLING TREES

☛ If you have a small, unwanted or dangerous tree in the garden, it is feasible to chop it down yourself. Don't just get the chainsaw out and hack the tree off at the base – this is very dangerous. You'll need a ladder, a big bow-saw, a lopper, an axe, a shovel and a length of rope. Begin by getting rid of the small branches, using the lopper, to thin out the mass. Then, starting at the top of the tree, take the bow-saw and cut off the larger branches one by one. Now, from the top, cut through the main trunk in 1-m (3-ft) sections, leaving at least 2 m (6 ft) still standing. Now dig a 60-cm (2-ft) trench around the base of the tree and cut through the roots, using the shovel blade if they're thin and an axe if they're not. Tie the rope around the top of the trunk and heave. You should have sufficient leverage to pull the tree to the ground. If the tree is big – that is, if you can't safely reach the highest branches by standing on a ladder – call in the professionals.

WARNING

☛ Some trees are protected. Check with the relevant authorities before felling.

☛ Warn neighbours before felling, to keep them from wandering into the danger area.

☛ Do not sit or lean on a branch that you are cutting through!

Casting your own stepping stones

67

CONCRETE IS marvellous stuff — I'm a real convert! It's cheap, readily available and easy to mix, and the result is extremely durable and sturdy. However, it's also a bit heavy, so don't be too ambitious with size when you consider this project. The basic principle runs like this: make a mould, pour in the concrete mix, wait until it sets and remove the mould...easy. I've chosen a simple heart shape but you can just as easily create a mould of your own, like a giant biscuit cutter. The mould is reusable, so you can cast as many stepping stones as you need.

TIP
Ask your local metal supplier to cut a piece of aluminium to size.

need

* pencil and tracing paper
* marker pen
* sharp kitchen knife
* ready-mix dry concrete
* old bucket
* wooden batten to mix the concrete and tamp the mould
* rubber mallet
* disposable latex gloves
* work gloves
* 45-cm (18-in) square sheet of thick polystyrene
* strip of thin aluminium, about 10 cm x 120 cm (4 in x 47 in)
* duct tape
* release agent (light oil spray, such as WD-40; cooking oil will do)

1 Trace the heart-shaped template on page 183. Put on the work gloves and bend the aluminium strip to match the shape of the template. Tape the ends together with duct tape. Trace the outline of the shape on to the polystyrene sheet, then cut a groove along it with the kitchen knife to accommodate the edge of the metal shape.

2 Place the metal heart on to the polystyrene sheet and press the lower edge firmly into the cut groove. Wear the gloves for this – the metal edges can be sharp.

3 Take the batten and place it across the top of the mould, then bang the batten with the rubber mallet to make sure the mould is firmly embedded in the polystyrene. Spray the inside of the mould with oil; this acts as a release agent so that the concrete won't stick.

4 Place about one-third of the dry concrete mix into an old bucket. Read the instructions on the package carefully. Pour in the correct amount of water over the dry mix as indicated in the instructions and mix thoroughly using the batten.

* WHY ON EARTH DOES EVERYBODY CALL ME HARD-HEARTED HANNAH?

5 Pour the wet mixture into the mould; it should be wet enough to level itself. Now tap the sides of the mould to release any air bubbles in the mixture.

6 Put on the latex gloves and trace a swirl pattern (or a design of your choice) in the surface of the concrete using your index finger. Don't take too long because the mixture begins to set in about thirty minutes. Set the mould aside for a day or two.

TIP

One 25-kg (55-lb) bag of concrete mix will make about three stepping stones of this size and about 6 cm (1½ in) deep.

TIP

Be sure to add the correct amount of water to the dry mix; the set mortar may be weakened if the mixture is overwatered.

7 You can now remove the metal heart mould; the concrete should be sufficiently hard not to need the mould. Remove the concrete stepping stone and set aside for a few more days until completely set. The mould is now ready for reuse, so you can make as many stones as you like.

One small step...

SETTING STEPPING STONES

Stepping stones are less obtrusive than a solid pathway, and more decorative. Use them to lead to a cute bench in a sunny spot, or to a focal point, such as a pond or sundial. You could have pretty stepping stones leading to the garden shed, simply for your own amusement! The other point to note is, of course, cost. A continuous solid pathway can be expensive; a few stepping stones serve the same purpose for a fraction of the cost. In addition, a few well-placed stepping stones can act as lawn savers; instead of laying a solid pathway, just set the stones along the track that gets walked on most often.

TIP
Functionality need not be the main purpose of a stepping stone. You can buy or make decorative shapes that serve as focal points in themselves. You don't really have to step on them at all!

✳ WALK ON WET GRASS? IN THESE SHOES? WHAT ARE YOU THINKING?

❶ Lay all the stepping stones along the intended route. Make sure that you space them evenly; an easy pace apart will be about right, so that you don't have to take tiny steps or leap from one stone to the next like a gazelle. Walk along the pathway and make any adjustments before setting the stones.

❷ When you're completely happy with the positioning of the stepping stones, use the point of a trowel to cut through the turf around the edge of the first stone. Ensure that you make quite a deep cut so you will be able to remove the topsoil without too much trouble.

❸ Now remove the stone and lay it near its intended position. If you're using natural or irregular stones, then it probably won't fit in another hole.

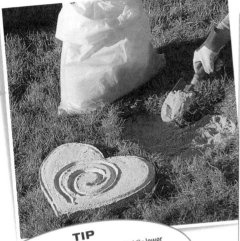

TIP

Ensure stepping stones' surfaces are slightly lower than the surrounding ground so that your lawn mower will just skim over the top and path users won't trip.

need

* stepping stones
* gloves
* trowel
* shovel
* sharp sand
* hand trowel
* spirit level
* tamping board
* mallet

Sharp sand

4 Remove the turf patch within the cut outline. The aim is to excavate the soil underneath to accommodate the depth of the stone plus a 2.5-cm (1-in) bed of sand. The sand helps keep the stone level and firm. Ideally, the surface of the stone should be slightly lower than the surrounding ground.
The reasons for this are twofold: to save your lawn mower and to help pathway users! If the stone juts out of the lawn, then the mower blades may be damaged and pedestrians may trip over the edge and fall.

5 Excavate each hole using a small hand trowel, then fill with sand to a depth of about 2.5 cm (1 in). Tamp across the surface with the end of the wooden board so that it is roughly level. The levelling process is helped if the sand is slightly damp. If you find that your sand is too dry, simply spray with water using a plant spray after placing the board in the hole, then tamp down.

6 Lay the stones in the prepared holes, then walk along the path, checking each one to see whether it rocks or remains steady. When you reach a wobbly stepping stone, place the board across its top and tap gently with the mallet to even out the sand packing underneath and stabilize the stone.

PEST CONTROL

Slugs and snails – they will eat everything in sight. Slug pellets are unpleasant but effective, but my favoured method is the slug trap – yes, a good old-fashioned one. Bury a dish in the soil and fill it with beer. The slugs will be attracted to it, fall in and drown – simple. There's always the option of the midnight vigil: stay up late, go outside with a torch, find all the slugs and snails that have come out to play, and pick them up (with gloves on!). Dispose of in a manner of your choosing.

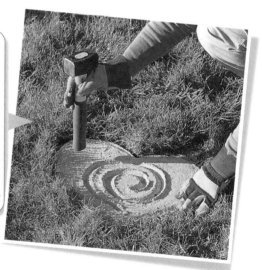

BROADS! YOU GIVE 'EM YOUR HEART AND THEY JUST WALK ALL OVER IT!

Making a bottle-bottom path

69

YOU'VE THROWN a party and your friends have kindly left you with lots of empty bottles. What can you do with them? Well, you can put them in a box and take them to the local recycling facility, or you can get creative in the garden. Small glass bottles make perfect edgings for pathways or flower beds — all you have to do is soak them in water to remove the labels, then decide where you'd like the pathway or edge to go. Gravel paths are also a good solution if the ground is uneven. No need to use the spirit level for this one!

* I GUESS I CAN DOWN A FEW MORE IF YOU REALLY NEED MORE BOTTLES.

1 Decide the location of your path, then mark roughly with wooden battens if the pathway is straight or with pegs and string to indicate curves. Use the fork to loosen the soil a little in the section between the strings. Using a hand trowel, dig narrow trenches on either side of the pathway to accommodate the beer bottles, just inside the strings.

2 Place the bottles in a row, neck-down in the trenches. Place the batten across the base of each one and strike a few times with the rubber mallet to make sure the bottle is firmly embedded in the earth. The base of each bottle should protrude above ground level by about 5 cm (2 in) on each side of the pathway.

TIP
You can use wine bottles for this, too, but you need to dig a deeper trench to fit them in.

3 Take the batten and use it to tamp down the soil between the bottle edges. The earth does not need to be absolutely level, so you can march up and down the path in your wellies and let your feet do all the tamping. The soil needs to be about 6 cm (2½ in) below ground level to accommodate the sand layer and the gravel.

TIP

You can use landscaping material under the sand layer if you like. This helps to prevent weed growth.

need

* lots of empty glass beer bottles
* fork
* hand trowel
* bricklayer's sand
* gravel
* wooden batten
* rubber mallet
* rake
* spade

4 Carefully empty a few bags of bricklayer's sand on to the tamped earth and use the batten or a rake to spread the sand out evenly.

TIP

Bags of sand and gravel are quite weighty. Always approach heavy loads carefully, lifting from the knees so that you don't injure your back.

5 Now it's time for more tamping with that batten, or marching up and down briskly if you prefer. For your path to look even, the sand layer needs to be of a reasonably uniform thickness: about 3 cm (1¼ in) should be sufficient.

6 Finally, pour on the gravel layer. There are many types of gravel available in all sorts of colours and sizes – just take your pick. Use a garden rake to spread the gravel evenly over the path. Don't worry if the sand and gravel layers settle a little after a short period of time; you can simply level them up again with more gravel at a later date.

WHAT! YOU WANT ME TO DO ANOTHER ONE?

Welcome aboard

INSTALLING DECKING

70

Everybody wants a deck these days, whether it is a high-level deck to even out a garden gradient and create a new outdoor living platform or a low-level deck as an alternative to a patio. No special skills are needed and all the materials are relatively inexpensive and readily available at DIY stores.

PROJECT CONSIDERATIONS

What and where? Basically, decks fall into two categories: high-level and low-level. Use the basic low-level construction for flat areas, and high-level or part-raised decks for sloping gardens.

PREPARING THE SITE

Mark out the proposed deck area with a bricklayer's line and pegs. Remove any turf from the area and make sure that flat areas

✻ SEE WHAT HAPPENS WHEN YOU SEND A MAN TO DO A WOMAN'S JOB!

are levelled out completely. To keep any unwanted plant life from growing through the deck, lay landscaping material over the site and cover with gravel if you choose.

BASIC FRAMEWORK AND JOIST POSITIONING

A deck basically consists of a timber frame around the perimeter spanned by supporting joists. Ideally, the joists should be no more that 40 cm (16 in) apart. The framework must be supported from underneath by timber sole plates, which in turn are supported by solid concrete footings sunk into the ground.

SUPPORTING THE DECK

DECKING BOARDS

JOIST

FASCIA BOARD ATTACHED TO END OF JOISTS

SOLE PLATE

CONCRETE FOOTING

PIERS OF BRICKS OR BLOCKS

☞ You'll need concrete pads in each corner and at about 1.5-m (5-ft) intervals around the perimeter, and perhaps in the middle, to ensure that no part of the deck framework comes into contact with the ground. Mark the position of each footing, then dig out a 30-cm (12-in) square hole at each point. Fill with a 6:1 ballast-cement concrete mix, then allow it to set. Build platforms on each concrete footing, using a few bricks and mortar. Use a long plank and a spirit level to ensure that the platforms or 'piers' are all level with each other. Now lay the wooden sole plates across the piers and nail the deck joists to the plates where they cross.

DECKING BOARDS

☞ Although you can use ordinary tanalized timber planks as decking boards (they need to be at least 25 mm/1 in thick), many timber yards and garden centres sell specially-made decking boards. These have several grooves machined in their top surface to help water run-off and ensure a good grip underfoot.

BASIC LOW-LEVEL DECKING

LOW LEVEL DOESN'T MEAN LOW QUALITY!

The basic support and framework construction is identical for high-level decking. The only difference is that the whole thing is raised on posts, securely anchored to concrete piers. The decking boards can span the joists at ninety degrees for a horizontal arrangement or you can go for a diagonal arrangement (but this means lots of cutting with the jigsaw).

1 To create the basic deck framework, simply cut four joists to fit the perimeter of the proposed site, then nail together at the corners. Make sure that the corners are perfectly square, unless of course you are building a deck to fit an irregular shape. These four joists will form the front, back and sides of the deck, and will provide a sturdy frame to which the floor joists and deck boards are secured.

2 Now cut floor joists to span the framework, slot them between the front and back framework joists at intervals of no more than 40 cm (16 in), then treat all cut ends with wood preservative.

3 Screw the joists to the framework using pre-drilled and countersunk screw holes. Use three screws per joist end.

4 Cut the boards to size and apply wood preservative to the cut ends. Drill and countersink all screw holes in the joists. Place the first board flush with the face of the front joist and screw in place. Position the next board, leaving a gap of about 3 mm (⅛ in). Continue until the entire area is covered.

5 Use some decking boards as fascia panels to conceal the cut ends of the basic wooden framework. Simply cut the boards to size, drill and countersink the screw holes as before, then screw into position.

DIAGONAL ARRANGEMENT

HORIZONTAL ARRANGEMENT

need

* drill and bits
* dust mask
* gloves and goggles
* saw and jigsaw
* spade
* hammer
* decking boards
* measuring tape and spirit level
* bricklayer's line and pegs
* cement and ballast for footing
* 100-mm x 50-mm (4-in x 2-in) tanalized timber for the deck sole plates
* 150-mm x 50-mm (6-in x 2-in) tanalized timber for joists
* 150-mm (6-in) galvanized nails
* screwdriver and 50-mm (2-in) screws

Keeping it all shipshape on deck

71

FINISHING AND WEATHERPROOFING DECKING

Weatherproofing your beautiful new deck is extremely important if you want the fruit of your hard labour to continue to look good in years to come. There are a great many clear sealing or staining/sealing products on the market now; choose a natural wood tone or a colour to match your garden furniture. It is a better idea to choose a penetrating stain if you decide you want colour, because paint tends to crack and peel eventually. Stains or sealants are easily applied using a large brush or roller with a long handle.

✽ WOOD STAIN IS NICE, BUT I'M PARTIAL TO PINK!

need

* roller with long handle or large paintbrush
* paint kettle or roller tray
* stiff brush
* sealer or stain

1 Sweep the deck with a stiff brush to remove dust and dirt. It is advisable to scrub the deck with a mild solution of detergent to remove any previous finish. Allow the wood to dry before applying stain or sealants.

DON'T DO THIS IN YOUR FANCY SHOES!

2 When the decking boards are dry, apply an even coat of stain or sealant, using a large brush or roller. Pour the product into a paint kettle or roller tray.

3 It is important not to load the brush/roller too heavily since this may result in pools forming on the surface. Remember to treat any exposed board ends with the same stain or sealant. If you do discover a pool or two, just spread out the excess with a clean brush. Do not allow the pool to dry or you'll get a patchy finish.

DECK MAINTENANCE

Regular maintenance will keep your deck looking great. All it takes is a little time every now and then to remove debris and dirt build-up. Your deck will, if taken care of properly, last for years.

need

* rubber gloves
* bucket
* scrubbing brush
* small hand brush
* scraper
* hosepipe

1 Sweep the deck to remove any loose dirt and debris, then get to work with a scraper. Slide the blade of the scraper down between the decking boards to hook out any matter that may have lodged itself in there. Any blockages in the gaps between the boards may cause water to collect, eventually giving rise to rot.

2 Choose a good-quality deck cleaning product, put your gloves on and get to work. Pour the cleaner into a large paint kettle, then apply it to the deck surface with a stiff scrubbing brush. Work the product into the boards, scrubbing away the dirt.

3 Hose down the entire deck now to wash away all the suds, taking all the dirt and grime with them. Begin cleaning close to the house, then work your way out towards the edge of the deck.

They call this fatigue duty in the navy!

TIP
When using the pressure washer, cover up any plants or shrubs nearby to prevent damage to foliage. Use a light plastic tarpaulin for this.

4 If the deck has been neglected for some time, it may well be very dirty or have lots of algae build-up. Use your low-pressure washer to clean it thoroughly. Remember to wear your wellies or you'll get wet feet! Allow the surface to dry before reapplying any finish. It's best to do a job like this on a warm, sunny day.

How to make a big entrance

MAKING WOODEN STEPS UP AND DOWN TO DECKING

75

If you'd like to create an access stairway to a high-level deck or make steps to join different decking levels, then you can easily do so. Wooden deck stair strings are readily available from DIY stores and garden centres. Strings are the shaped side panels that are cut to follow the rise and run lines, and provide support for the treads (the horizontal parts). All you have to do is attach the strings to the deck, secure them to paving slabs or a concrete pad in the ground, then use deck boards for the treads.

✴ WHY DON'T YOU COME UP AND SEE ME SOMETIME?

COME ON UP! **INSTALLING STEPS**

- ANGLE BRACKET
- TREAD
- COACH SCREW
- ANGLE BRACKET
- FASCIA
- STRING
- CONCRETE PAD

1 Decide on the position of the steps and the area for the paving slabs or concrete pad. Either mark out the area on the ground with a line and pegs or just place the slabs on the ground and cut into the earth all round with a trowel. Excavate the turf and soil to a depth of about 7.5 cm (3 in), then compact the earth with a board. Mix the concrete and water according to the package directions, then pour into the shallow hole. Level the surface with the board, then allow the mix to set. For the slabs, lay a 2.5-cm (1-in) layer of sand in the hole. Then place the slabs on top.

2 Decide on the width of the steps and cut the decking boards to that measurement to make the treads. Treat all cut ends with wood preserver.

3 Drill and countersink screw holes in the ends of the treads, then screw each to the strings.

4 Now use the angle brackets to secure the top of the wooden strings to the fascia board of the deck, and the base to the concrete pad/paving slabs. Drill the holes in the slabs or concrete pad with a masonry drill, insert plugs, then drive in the screws.

need

- ✴ two wooden strings
- ✴ decking boards for treads
- ✴ drill with bits and countersink bit
- ✴ saw
- ✴ screwdriver
- ✴ screws
- ✴ wall plugs
- ✴ four angle brackets
- ✴ paving slabs or ready-mix dry concrete
- ✴ shovel
- ✴ sand

REPAIRING CONCRETE STEPS

Over time, concrete steps may sustain damage due to wear and weather. This may result in cracking, flaking or a general unevenness in the surface of the step, which in time can become dangerous and unsightly. Check steps periodically to make sure they are sound and safe. When the new concrete is dry, paint the whole flight with a non-slip floor paint so the repair doesn't show.

need

* wooden board
* saw
* few bricks
* club hammer
* brick bolster
* trowel
* float
* goggles
* PVA adhesive
* paintbrush
* ready-mix concrete
* old bucket and batten
* thin sheet of metal
* short wooden batten
* screws

* SAY, DORIS, JAKE'S GOT HIS VERY OWN CLUB HAMMER!

* IS THAT ALL YOU WOMEN EVER THINK ABOUT?

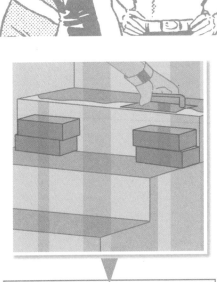

1 Put on your gloves and safety goggles. Using the brick bolster and club hammer, carefully chip away any loose material from the repair area to make the base stable. Cut the wooden board to fit the riser of the step to be repaired and prop it in place with a few bricks. Apply PVA solution to the repair area using a paintbrush.

2 Following the manufacturer's instructions, mix a small amount of concrete and water in the bucket using the batten. Scoop up the mixture with a trowel and drop it into the repair area behind the board. Use the float to smooth out the surface and sides so they are flush with the edges of the board and the rest of the step.

3 To round off the edge before the concrete sets, bend a piece of metal over the edge of a table to make an L-shape. Screw the short batten to the horizontal side as a makeshift handle. Slip the vertical side of the metal between the concrete and the wooden board. Slide it along the step to the other side. This will soften and round off the sharp edge.

FENCING LESSONS

Whether you own acres of land or a tiny garden, you'll need to build and repair fences — read on to find out what to do and how.

How to keep those wide open spaces in their place!

Do fence me in

Decorative or functional, your fences should be well maintained, look lovely and serve the purpose for which they are intended. One important thing to remember is — the neighbours! Check with neighbours on either side first before starting a fence project. You'll also need to check with neighbours if the new fence is to be higher or more substantial than the old one — it may block out light in their garden. Finally, find out if there are any restrictions imposed by local authorities — be a considerate fencer!

REPLACING A BOARD IN A FENCE

Closeboard fencing is probably the simplest type of fence. It is made by nailing vertical feather-edge boards to horizontal timber rails that are mortised into vertical fence posts. Each overlaps its neighbour and can be finished by adding a capping strip along the top edge. The result is an attractive solid fence panel. Softwood is the favoured material for such fences because it is plentiful and cheap. Apply wood preservative or a stain to replacement boards — match the old boards as closely as possible or change the whole fence to fit in with the general garden decor.

need

* feather-edge boards
* tenon saw
* pencil
* wood preservative
* paintbrush
* galvanized nails
* claw hammer

1 Remove all loose or damaged boards and discard them. If the wood is rotten, then it isn't worth trying to save it. Hang on to ones that are not damaged. Now remove any old nails with the claw part of your hammer. Use one of the old boards to mark the length needed on the new boards, then saw each one to the correct size.

2 It is important that the freshly cut ends of each new board are treated with wood preservative. You can stain new boards to match the old fence after they have been secured. For a change of colour, clean up the old boards, then apply your new stain or paint.

3 Feather-edge boards are tapered towards one long side, that is, they have one thick edge and one thin one. The general rule is that you work from left to right, keeping the thick edge on the left. The next board should overlap the thin edge of the previous one by about 12 mm (½ in). Space each board to match the old ones. Use sturdy galvanized nails to secure it to the cross rails, making sure that it doesn't pierce the boards underneath.

CLEANING FENCES

Eventually everything gets dirty, especially outdoor stuff! Exposed to the elements all year round, fences can accumulate dirt, grime and algae growth, which, if left untreated, can lead to more serious damage, especially in the case of wooden fences. There's just no alternative but to get the gloves on and start the clean-up operation. It's not a hard task, a little time-consuming maybe, but well worth the effort. If you've got a lot of wooden fencing, it's worth investing in a pressure washer, although they are fairly inexpensive to hire. Once you've used one of these wonderful machines, you'll never look back (they're good for patios, walls, decks and windows, too!).

need

* rubber gloves
* bucket
* bleach (optional)
* sodium bicarbonate-based cleaner
* scrubbing brush
* cloth
* pressure washer
* hosepipe
* detergent
* wellingtons

A CLEAN FENCE MEANS A BRIGHTER GARDEN!

WOODEN FENCE

1 Use a pressure washer to remove stubborn stains or unsightly algae growth, especially on interwoven or overlapping fence panels. Put on your wellingtons before beginning because the water goes everywhere!

2 To achieve the best results, hold the nozzle of the pressure washer about 20 cm (8 in) away from the surface to be cleaned. The pressure washer reaches parts that a scrubbing brush or cloth cannot.

AND

1 If you don't have a pressure washer, you can clean a moderately dirty wooden fence with a household scrubbing brush. Fill a bucket with warm soapy water and scrub the wooden surface briskly – add a little bleach to the soapy water for very stubborn stains. Rinse the area with fresh water when you've finished. Do this on a warm, dry day so that the wood dries out properly, then you can paint or stain on the same day to complete the job.

MORE CLEANING!!!

UPVC FENCE

It's very important not to use a hard brush on UPVC surfaces. The bristles of a scrubbing or wire brush will scratch the plastic and cause permanent damage to the fence, so use a soft cloth instead. Before cleaning, it's a good idea to cover any surrounding plants with a plastic sheet to protect them. Use a solution of warm water and a household cleaner, which should remove all but the most stubborn dirt and stains. Do not be tempted to use any kind of bleach on UPVC fences because this may cause staining.

METAL FENCE

Cleaning a metal fence involves a tougher approach – a dirty or weatherworn metal fence needs the wire-brush treatment. First of all, protect any surrounding plants or foliage with a plastic sheet. Scrub the fence briskly all over with a solution of warm soapy water in order to remove dirt build-up and also to get rid of any flaking paint or rust patches. When it is dry, the metal can be treated with a rust inhibitor and repainted so that it looks as good as new.

Your very own little house on the prairie

MAKING OR REPAIRING A PICKET FENCE

76

Picket fences are very cute and have a wonderfully traditional appeal — especially when painted white. I have some along the wall of my front garden just ready and waiting for the paintbrush. Garden centres sell pre-cut palings in various lengths and designs, as well as ready-made fence panels. But it's easy to make your own palings for small repairs or to make a panel to fit a small or oddly shaped area.

need

* lengths of 75-mm x 25-mm (3-in x 1-in) timber
* pencil
* rule
* tenon saw
* abrasive paper
* drill and countersink bit
* screwdriver and screws

1 Cut two cross rails to fit across the damaged area or between existing fence posts. Now cut the palings to the size needed. At one end of each, use a pencil to mark the centre, then mark a point approximately 5 cm (2 in) down each side from the top. Connect the three dots with straight lines to form a triangle.

2 Saw carefully along the pencil lines, then sand all the rough cut edges smooth. It is important that the points are smooth and free of splinters, not just for appearance's sake, but as a safety precaution in case someone should run their hand along the top of the fence.

3 Mark the intended position of the cross rail on each of the palings with a pencil. Make two screw holes set diagonally at the point where the cross rail meets each paling. At a butt joint, make two holes at each end of both pieces, making four in total. Countersink each screw hole so that the screw head will lie flush with the surface of the wood.

TIP
To replace a paling, simply cut one the same size as the damaged one and screw in position. It is a good idea to make new screw holes in the cross rails and not use the old ones.

4 Screw each paling securely to the cross rail (make a clearance hole in the cross rail first). Use screws instead of nails to avoid splitting the wood, but if you must, blunt the point of the nail first by tapping it with a hammer. If there are to be joints in the cross rails, butt the ends together halfway across a fence post or paling.

MAMA SAYS YOU SHOULDN'T PICKET OR IT'LL NEVER GET BETTER!

CHEAT!

ATTACHING READY-MADE PICKET PANELS

It is possible to buy ready-made picket fence panels. Measure the area carefully and make sure you purchase enough for your needs. It's better to have too many than too few – most DIY stores will exchange or refund cash for goods if they are returned unused, so keep your receipts. Cut the panels to fit between existing fence posts or set new ones in concrete (*see page 147*). Hold up the picket panels to the fence posts and mark with pencil lines the position of the cross rails top and bottom. Screw two metal brackets to each post, then screw on the picket panels.

RANCH-STYLE FENCING

HOME, HOME ON THE RANGE!

RAIL JOINTS   SHORT POSTS

HORIZONTAL RAILS

Ranch-style post-and-rail fencing serves well as a low-level boundary where no privacy is required – or where there are no small children or pets to keep in! Simply screw horizontal cross rails to existing fence posts, or set new ones in concrete (*see page 147*). Butt the cross rails together halfway across a fence post. Also, make sure that the joints are staggered – don't place all the joints on one post. This way there won't be any weak spots in the fence construction.

TIP
If mending or replacing a portion of cross rail, then reinforce the joint with a metal fixing bracket.

Does your entrance let you down?

REHANGING A GATE

A broken or damaged gate is so annoying. Mine was hung with steel hinges that quickly became rusty and eventually seized up completely, causing the gate post on the hinge side to work loose. The only answer is to use brass hinges and screws. They're a little more expensive than steel ones, but they won't rust and you'll save yourself time and effort in the future.

1 Remove all the old rusty hinges and any other fittings, such as the gate latch, and discard them. If it is a particularly bad case of rust, then you may have to work really hard to get the screws out. If you're having trouble, try tapping the head of the screw first, then unscrew it – this can loosen it up a bit.

2 Locate the screws holding the post to the wall. Tighten the screws first to see if that holds the post more solidly to the wall. If this has no effect, you may have to remove the gate post and insert new wall plugs into the old holes, or possibly drill new holes in the wall and through the post and reattach it.

3 It is unlikely that the holes of the new hinge will correspond with the old screw holes, so fill all the old screw holes with a good-quality exterior wood filler, allow to set, then sand smooth.

4 Screw the new hinge to the gate first, then hold up the gate to the old post. Use the wooden wedges or prop up the gate with battens so it is raised to the correct height. Drill pilot holes first, then screw the hinge securely to the post. Insert the top and bottom screws first to keep the gate in position while the remaining screws are inserted.

5 Finally, close the gate in order to attach the new gate latch. Place the latch part on the post and mark the screw holes with a bradawl. Do the same with the bar part on the gate. Screw both parts in place.

need

* screwdriver
* brass hinges with screws
* exterior-quality wood filler
* new gate latch
* bradawl
* thin wooden wedges (or battens to hold gate level when rehingeing)

MAKING A GATE

If your garden gate is damaged beyond repair, then the best thing to do is discard it and make a nice new one. You'll find softwood gate kits like this in DIY stores. When you open up the kit, read the instructions carefully and familiarize yourself with the pieces before you begin. A clear diagram will identify each component and the instructions will indicate which screw or fixing to use at each stage.

need

* screwdriver
* saw
* hammer
* nail punch
* wood glue
* measuring tape
* pencil

1 Determine the width of the gate. Cut the bottom rail to this width and the top rail 14 cm (5½ in) shorter. Position the bottom rail in the cut-outs in the hinge and latch posts. Make sure that the rail ends are flush with the post edges.

2 Secure the rails with the screws provided. Position the end of the top rail that has drilled pilot holes between the hinge and latch posts. Then screw through the holes in the posts to secure the rail at each end.

3 Lay the assembly on the cross brace, then mark the pointed shape at each end using a pencil. Mark also the position of the cross brace on the top and bottom rail. The bottom end of the cross brace must always be on the hinge-post side. Cut carefully along the pencil lines. Apply wood glue to the marked areas on the top and bottom rails, then reposition the cross brace.

4 Place the vertical slats on the assembly and space out as needed. Mark the position of each slat with faint pencil lines on the top and bottom rail and the cross brace, then remove the slats. Apply wood glue to the marked areas, reposition each slat and attach with nails. Use a nail punch to drive the nail heads below the surface. Wipe away excess glue and let dry.

CURING A SQUEAKY GATE

Hinges have a tendency to get squeaky and creaky over time, especially if they are situated outdoors — annoying for you and your neighbours. The simple answer is to keep the hinges well lubricated. A drop of oil every now and then will ensure that the hinges are fully operational and, above all, nice and quiet!

ALL GIRLS APPRECIATE A SMOOTH OPERATOR!

Divide and rule

INSTALLING A PANEL FENCE

80

Ready-made panel fences are easy to put up, making them a popular choice as a quick and cheap fencing option. Normally available in a standard 1.8-m (6-ft) width in a variety of different heights, they may be overlapping or interwoven in style. The panels are normally already treated, so are ready to stain if you desire. Panels like these provide a solid and durable screen, and are ideal for use where a degree of privacy is required.

1 Mark the position of the fence using a line and pegs. Drive in a metal fence spike at one end of the marked line. Place a small block of wood in the socket of the fencing spike to avoid damaging the spike when you drive it in. The block should be taller than the depth of the socket but smaller than the fence-post dimension – this is to keep it from becoming stuck in the socket. Drive the spike into the ground using the sledgehammer, making sure it is set square to the marked fence line.

2 Cut each fence post to size, that is, the height of the fence panel plus the depth of the spike socket plus a little extra to protrude at the top. Remove the wooden block from the spike, and insert the new fence post. Use a spirit level to check that the post is vertical. Mark the position of the next spike, the width of a fence panel from the first, then insert the spike in the same way.

3 Attach two fence-panel clips to each fence post using galvanized nails, one at the top and the other at the bottom. If it is a tall panel then you could use one in the middle as well. Slot the fence panels into position, then screw the clips to the panel.

4 To finish each post, attach a shaped wooden post cap. Simply drive two galvanized nails through the cap into the top of the post. This is not absolutely necessary, but it's a nice finishing touch and gives a professional appearance.

need

* fence posts
* fence panels
* metal fence-post spikes
* line and pegs
* sledgehammer
* hammer
* spirit level
* saw
* post clips
* screws
* fence-post caps
* galvanized nails

SETTING A POST IN CONCRETE

As an alternative to using metal fence spikes, you can set fence posts in concrete. You can also use this method to anchor a metal washing-line post firmly in the ground.

need

* fence post
* post-setting mix
* fence-post digger
* spirit level
* watering can

AND

ERECTING A PANEL FENCE ON A SLOPE

1 Dig a hole about 30 cm (12 in) in diameter. The depth should be about one-third of the finished height of the fence. Use a fence-post digger, or a fence-post auger for this task. You can hire both quite cheaply. Allow plenty of time to do this so that you don't feel tempted to take shortcuts.

2 Ram a layer of ballast in the bottom of the hole and tamp down hard. This will provide a firm base and also allow ample drainage. Now drop the post into the hole and fill the surrounding gap with the concrete mix to about 5 cm (2 in) below the soil level.

3 Following the manufacturer's instructions, carefully pour the correct amount of water on to the dry mix using a watering can. At this point, check with a spirit level to ensure that the post is truly vertical, and brace with wooden stakes if necessary while the concrete sets.

☞ If your garden has even a slight downward slope, it will be necessary to set the panels in a series of little 'steps' to accommodate the gradient. Mark out the position of the fence with a line and pegs in the usual way, then mark each fence-spike position. Each fence post must be set vertically as before, but must be longer to allow for the slope in the ground. The shallow, triangular-shaped gaps that will appear between the bottom of the fence panels and the ground can be filled in with retaining walls.

Join the chain gang

ADJUSTING A METAL-POST, CHAIN-LINK FENCE

82

Chain-link fences are typically built with metal end posts that have special straining-wire winding brackets and right-angle intermediate posts at intervals in between. The straining wires that support the mesh are attached to the end posts by means of a winding bracket; each intermediate post has holes through which the wires pass on their way to the other end post. Over time, the wire mesh in these fences may become detached from the straining wires and lose its tautness and shape. Follow the steps opposite to get it back into shape again.

need
* gloves
* pliers
* adjustable spanner or locking pliers
* galvanized clips

1 If the chain-link mesh has become detached from the straining wires, you can straighten out the mesh and then reattach it to the wires in one of two ways. Either use short lengths of galvanized wire twisted together, or you can just straighten out the top links of the mesh and then hook them round the wires. Use pliers to squeeze the hook shapes together, holding the mesh securely.

2 If the fence is more than around 1 m (3 ft) high, the mesh will need to be attached to a third straining wire located at the mid-point. This will keep the fence from losing its shape. Use twisted wire or small galvanized clips to secure.

3 Finally, check the tension of the straining wires. Tighten the wire winding brackets using an adjustable spanner or locking pliers. At each end post there will be a vertical stretcher bar that is passed through the end links of the mesh, keeping the panel straight. Make sure that the nuts and bolts of the attachments are secure – this may be hard work if the mechanism has been painted over, or has rusted.

* CALL ME OLD-FASHIONED, BUT SHOULDN'T THIS FENCE BE A BIT HIGHER?

REPAIRING A WOOD-POST, CHAIN-LINK FENCE

83

Chain-link fencing on wooden fence posts needs regular maintenance. The fencing is supported on two or more thick straining wires attached to end posts by means of straining bolts. These bolts are passed through the post, then secured with nuts. The end of each wire is tied to the eye of a bolt. The wires are stapled to intermediate line posts and secured to bolts in the other end post. Adjust the nut of each bolt to tension the straining wires. If the basic wire mesh is sound but has come loose, you can easily straighten it out and replace the staples.

❋ THIS IS ANOTHER FINE MESH YOU'VE GOT ME INTO!

1 Examine the whole length of fence and locate any loose parts. Secure the mesh to the horizontal straining wires at approximately 30-cm (12-in) intervals using short lengths of galvanized wire twisted together. Locate any loose or missing staples, then use long-nosed pliers to remove the loose ones.

2 If, over time, the fixing staples have worked loose, then the mesh will certainly come away from the posts, and so will probably crumple and become distorted. Just put on your protective gloves and grasp the mesh firmly. You can now stretch and straighten out any kinks or folds.

TIP
While you're mending or replacing the chain-link fence, you could take the opportunity to repaint or restain the wooden fence posts. If a job's worth doing, then it's worth doing well.

3 Secure each end link of the mesh panel to the end post using new galvanized staples – don't reuse the old ones. It's also a good idea not to reuse the old nail holes either because the new staples will easily work loose and fall out.

need
* gloves
* fence staples
* hammer
* long-nosed pliers
* galvanized wire

Protecting your territory

84

CHANGING A PORCH LIGHT TO A SECURITY LIGHT

An exterior wall or porch light is of more use to you and your visitors if it has a PIR (passive infra-red) motion sensor built in that will automatically switch the light on when it detects someone approaching the door. The light switching on will let you know that someone is out there — friend or foe!

need

- PIR security light
- ladder
- spanner
- screwdriver
- drill
- wall plugs
- hammer
- wire strippers
- pliers

1 Locate the old porch light. If you are using a ladder, make sure it is safe and on level ground before climbing up. Check the type of fixings on the old light. Make sure you have the right tool with you before you get up the ladder.

2 Unfasten the wall plate of the old light to expose the wires inside. You will see a plastic connecting block. Loosen the screws to release the wires – you can now remove the light.

3 Unscrew and remove the old base plate. Attach the new base plate securely to the wall, using the screws and wall plugs provided – the cable from the mains supply will pass through the base plate. Follow the instructions provided to connect the wiring correctly, then install the assembly securely in position. Switch on the power and test the light, adjusting the angle of the sensor to suit your needs.

WARNING

☞ Always make sure that the electricity is switched off at the main isolating switch before undertaking any electrical repairs or modifications. Do not dismantle electrical fittings without turning off the power to that fitting's circuit at the fuse box. If you need to use a power tool, then use a cordless one. Also, make sure you read the instructions provided with the appliance before you begin.

☞ If you're not lucky enough to have an existing exterior light fitting, and would like one installed, ask an electrician to do it for you. This also applies to power points in sheds, or installing weatherproof outdoor sockets.

SECURITY LIGHTS ARE ALSO USEFUL WHEN YOU ARE SEARCHING IN YOUR HANDBAG FOR THE DOOR KEYS, OR FOR GUESTS LOOKING FOR THE DOORBELL.

INSTALLING A SIMPLE WIRE-FREE ALARM

Lots of domestic alarm systems are totally wire-free and battery-operated! Most are purchased in kits with full instructions and test procedures provided. A basic kit includes an external siren, internal PIR motion sensors and wire-free door/window contact magnets.

1. The siren is mounted on an exterior wall — use the back plate as a template to mark mounting holes, then drill, plug and secure to the wall with screws.

2. The door/window contact magnets are fitted on either the fixed or the opening sections — position the magnet at the extreme edge of the door/window frame.

3. Mark the outline of the mounting bracket on the mounting surface, then screw it into position. When the window or door is opened it breaks the contact, which activates the siren.

4. Install PIR motion sensors on interior walls at around door height so that the sensor is directed across the room. When the device is switched on, the sensors will detect the presence of an intruder inside and activate the siren.

MOTION SENSORS USE MINIATURE RADIO TRANSMITTERS TO SET OFF THE ALARM.

ON GUARD
HOME SECURITY DANGER SPOTS

CHECK OUT ALL THE POSSIBLE MISTAKES!

LOCKS ON SHEDS AND OUTBUILDINGS

LOCK TOOLS AWAY

LOCKS ON ACCESSIBLE WINDOWS

DEADBOLT LOCKS TO DOORS

LOCK LADDERS AWAY

USE ANTI-CLIMB PAINT ON DOWNPIPES

Installing an alarm system will add to a feeling of security in your home, especially if you live alone. In addition, there may be many areas around your home that could potentially provide easy access for an intruder.

Perimeter fences and gates

Make sure all fences are in good repair. If you have a gate or door, ensure that it is in good working order and is lockable from the inside.

Doors and windows Make sure that all doors and windows have adequate locking systems. There are many products on the market designed to meet any number of security requirements. Doors should be fitted with mortised deadbolt locks, in addition to cylinder rimlocks. A burglar will happily break a window to get inside, but after doing so will want to open the window to avoid the broken glass – don't make it easy, install window locks!

MOTION SENSOR WITH CONTROL KEYPAD UNIT AND SIREN.

Making an art deco-style trellis

86

ON A RECENT visit to a garden centre I noticed how expensive simple trellis panels are! Rough-sawn wooden battens are extremely cheap to buy, so I thought I'd just go ahead and create my own. I took art deco architecture as my inspiration. Using an old mirror as a focal point, I added a little shelf to hold some votive candles — these produce a beautiful reflection in the mirror when lit in the evening. You can secure your trellis in a suitable place for use as a climbing-plant support, a garden divider or even a sunbathing screen. And try tying on a few fake flowers to the trellis just for fun!

1 Cut the battens into the lengths indicated opposite. Clear a bit of space in your garden and lay out the vertical pieces, allowing approximately 15 cm (6 in) between each (*see the constructional diagram on page 184*). Lay the horizontal pieces in position and you should see the trellis taking shape.

2 Nail the battens together at each corner and cross point. Now place the decorative fan shape in position at the top of the trellis and nail securely in place. The trellis should be quite solid and firm now, so pick it up carefully and turn it over.

3 Using the drill, make two holes on each side of the mirror frame, about 20 cm (8 in) from the upper and lower edges. Drive a screw through each of the holes to secure the mirror to the trellis frame. Now turn the trellis over again and lay flat as before.

GET YOUR MAN TO BUY THE FLOWERS!

4 Cut a piece of feather-edge board to fit across the bottom of the mirror between the vertical slats: this forms the candle shelf. Drill two small holes through the board close to the back edge and approximately 10 cm (4 in) from each end. Drive a screw through each hole to secure the shelf to the trellis.

TIP
To use as a plant support, screw vertical wooden battens to the wall first (drill holes in the wall, then plug as usual) and screw the trellis to them. This creates a gap between the wall and trellis, making it easier for climbing plants.

✳ MIRROR, MIRROR ON THE TRELLIS, WHO IS THE FAIREST? GO ON TELL US!

5 Lift the trellis into an upright position. You can attach it to a wall or use it as a garden divider mounted between fence posts (*see 'Installing a panel fence', page 146*).

TIP
Never leave burning candles unattended, especially if you have decorated your trellis with fake flowers!

6 Place a few votive candles on the shelf. The flames will reflect beautifully in the mirror.

𝓑asic pieces

Horizontals are numbered, verticals are lettered. See the diagram on page 184.

Horizontals

1: 48 cm/19 in (one)
2: 86 cm/34 in (one)
3: 125 cm/49 in (seven)
4: 40 cm/16 in (four)

Verticals

A: 150 cm/59 in (two)
B: 165 cm/65 in (two)
C: 180 cm/71 in (two)
D: 56 cm/22 in (three)

need

✳ 32-mm x 19-mm (1¼-in x ¾-in) rough-sawn battens
✳ piece of feather-edge fence board
✳ saw
✳ hammer
✳ 32-mm (1¼-in) nails
✳ drill
✳ brass screws
✳ old mirror, about 60 cm x 40 cm (24 in x 16 in)
✳ votive candles

MAKING IT GREAT OUTDOORS

Now that all the repairing, digging and fencing is done, get a little creative with garden accessories, furniture and features.

Finishing touches

Now that you've done all the serious work — digging, lopping, sawing and so on — it's time to have creative fun in the garden. This section covers all those finishing touches that make a real difference to the look of your garden, including re-covering a deck chair, hanging a hammock, painting and varnishing or weather-proofing wooden garden furniture, sprucing up plastic garden furniture, installing outdoor lighting and a water feature, cleaning and maintaining a barbecue and making a log store.

REPAIRING A GARDEN PARASOL

87

Re-covering a garden parasol is easy. Remove the old cover and use the pieces as templates for a new cover. Use the left-over fabric to make pockets or ties. Remember to use a heavy-duty needle in your sewing machine!

need

* canvas fabric
* sewing machine
* scissors, pins, thread
* teak oil
* cloth

1 Remove the old cover from the parasol frame and set aside. Clean any moving parts and wash the wood with soapy water. When dry, apply good teak or furniture oil to the surfaces with a soft cloth.

2 Cut out all the necessary shapes, including any pockets or ties, allowing about 12 mm (½ in) for the seam. All you have to do is use the old cover as a template for the new one. You can make paper patterns for the shapes, or simply cut the old cover into its component pieces and use them as templates.

3 (*See template diagram, page 184.*) Turn and stitch a narrow hem across the top and bottom edges of the four trapezoidal shapes. Pin and then machine stitch the main pieces together with the right side of the fabric facing upwards. Fold and stitch the corner and centre pockets into position. Turn and stitch a narrow hem around the top square flap, then secure this to the main part of the cover with fabric straps.

4 Unscrew the parasol finial at the top and slip on the new cover. Pass the top flap over the finial screw, then replace the finial. With the parasol closed, place the spoke ends into the corner and centre pockets. When opened, the cover should fit tightly.

RE-COVERING A DECK CHAIR

88

Have you got a few faded old deck chairs tucked away in the garden shed? Don't despair, and don't throw them away either — you can fix them up in no time! The deck-chair canvas already comes in the right width, so you don't even have to do any sewing or neatening of raw edges. How easy is that?

1 Use pincers to prise out all the old nails or tacks from the crossbars. Remove the old canvas and discard. At this point, it is a good idea to write a note on each crossbar, to remind yourself how to wrap the fabric!

2 Use abrasive paper to rub down the wooden framework. This removes any old paintwork or varnish and creates a good base for painting. When all the sanding is complete, wipe away dust particles using a cloth soaked in white spirit.

3 If you're decorating bare wood, apply a primer before the final paint finish. Primer sticks to the surface of the wood and ensures good adhesion for the top coat. After priming, apply one or two coats of exterior-quality gloss paint. Set the deck chair aside to dry. Some paints are self-priming, so you don't need to prime first with these.

STRIPES ONLY BELONG ON A DECK CHAIR!

4 Lay the painted frame face-down on your work surface. Using the notes that you made in step 1, wrap the end of the canvas strip around one crossbar twice, then use the staple gun to secure it. Pull the canvas taut, then wrap the free end around the other crossbar and staple to secure it to the crossbar.

need

* pincers
* abrasive paper
* white spirit
* cloth
* paintbrush
* primer
* exterior gloss paint
* 15 m (50 ft) of deck-chair canvas
* scissors
* staple gun

Making a hammock 89

OH YES! This is the life. Lazing in the garden after a hard day's work, shades on, cocktail in hand, magazine to read...lovely! To make this fabulous hammock, all you need is a length of heavy canvas (I chose a fantastic pink and red number), some eyelets and a piece of rope. One end of the hammock has a flap with fabric ties attached; just roll up the hammock when it's not in use, wrap the flap around it and tie it securely. It also helps if you have a nice, shady spot in your garden with a pair of trees from which to suspend the hammock! Getting in and out takes a bit of practice, but it's worth it in the end.

need

* about 3 m (10 ft) of brightly coloured canvas
* sewing machine and thread
* eyelet kit
* hammer
* two wooden broom handles
* saw
* needle
* strong rope

ESSENTIAL TOOL! A DRINKS TROLLEY.

1 Fold the fabric in half lengthways and then stitch the selvedges together to make a tube, taking a 12-mm (½-in) seam allowance. Press the seam flat, then refold the piece so that the seam runs down the centre of the tube. Stitch across one short end, then turn the fabric through to the right side, just like a big sleeping bag. Press it flat, then mark the eight eyelet-hole positions (*see template diagram, page 183*).

2 Following the instructions provided with the eyelet kit, insert eight metal eyelets at the positions marked. The kit contains a cutting tool and disc. Make a hole at each marked position using the cutting tool provided, then insert the upper and lower eyelet parts as instructed and hammer together to form the eyelet.

DON'T JUST STAND
THERE! BRING ME
A DRINK, WHY
DON'T YOU?

3 Next make the casings to hold the wooden supports. At the raw end, fold a 2-cm (¾-in) hem, then fold a further 10 cm (4 in) and pin in place. Make two rows of machine stitching close to the 2-cm (¾-in) hem. For the other end, fold back 33 cm (13 in). Pin in place and machine stitch two rows about 10 cm (4 in) from the fold.

4 Use the saw to cut the two wooden broom handles to size. Each should be around 5 cm (2 in) less than the measurement across the width of the hammock. Insert each broom-handle piece into the casing at each end of the hammock. Use matching thread to slip stitch over the openings at the ends of the casings.

6 Thread the ends of a 2-m (79-in) length of rope through the eyelets from the back to the front. Tie the ends of the rope together very securely – you don't want the knot to give way while you're relaxing.

5 For the ties, cut two 100-cm x 8-cm (40-in x 3-in) strips of fabric. Fold and press a narrow hem along the four edges of each strip, then fold in half lengthways. Machine stitch together, then stitch the ties to the edge of the flap as shown.

Sitting pretty in the garden

WEATHERPROOFING WOODEN GARDEN FURNITURE

90

There are two types of wooden garden furniture, softwood and hardwood, and both will deteriorate if left outside for any length of time. Cosmetic remedies are quick and easy, and with a little regular maintenance, your garden furniture will serve you well for many years. Fittings may be prone to rust; remove and treat with a rust-inhibiting product, then replace. It's a good idea to use brass or rustproof fittings and screws for outdoor furniture.

❶ Hardwood furniture loses its beautiful dark colour over time, becoming dull and grey. First scrub the framework thoroughly with soapy water and allow it to dry.

❷ Now use a cloth or brush to apply a coat of furniture oil to all the surfaces. This will replace the natural oils and keep the wood from drying out. Allow it to dry, then apply another coat. Rub with a clean cloth to remove excess oil, then leave for twenty-four hours before use. Do this twice a year to keep your garden furniture looking fantastic! Softwood can be cleaned, rubbed down, then revarnished or stained in a wood tone or colour.

* HEY, GIRLS! IF PLASTIC'S YOUR THING, THEN YOU'RE GONNA LOVE ME!

SPRUCING UP PLASTIC GARDEN FURNITURE

91

☞ Freshening up plastic furniture is easy. Use a specially formulated plastic-furniture spray cleaner and a soft cloth to remove dirt and grease. Some cleaning products contain ultraviolet stabilizers to prevent colours from fading. Avoid stiff brushes or abrasive cleaners, because they may scratch the plastic surface. It's a good idea to invest in furniture covers to protect your garden furniture when not in use.

TIP
Don't attempt to repair split or broken plastic garden furniture. Recycle it (ask at your local recycling centre) and buy some new stuff!

LOOKING AFTER METAL GARDEN FURNITURE

92

Metal furniture has a nasty habit of becoming rusty when left outside and exposed to dampness and adverse weather conditions. Prevention is better than cure, of course, but if you find yourself with a few corroded items, then it's a simple matter to de-rust and repaint them.

YUCK!
ALGAE GROWTH

Wrought-iron furniture weathers badly if left uncovered outdoors. Green algae can collect and grow in decorative nooks and crannies, not to mention the ever-present rust problem. The solution is easy. Scrub organic growth away with a stiff brush, use a fungicide to inhibit fresh growth, then follow the preparation, prime and paint routine given here.

Wear goggles to keep rust flakes from getting in your eyes.

1 Use a stiff wire brush to remove all loose flakes of paint and rust from the surface of the metal. Treat any wrought-iron furniture prone to algae growth as directed above, before painting.

2 Using a small paintbrush, apply a rust inhibitor to remove rust build-up and create a smooth surface for painting. Work the product into heavily affected areas. Some products remove rust completely, taking you back to the bare metal. Follow the manufacturer's instructions carefully when using these caustic products.

need
* wire brush
* rust inhibitor
* paintbrush
* abrasive paper
* anti-rust primer
* exterior paint suitable for metal
* white spirit
* cloth

3 When all rust-removing procedures are complete, rub down surfaces thoroughly using abrasive paper to create a smooth surface and a good key for painting. Wipe away all dust particles using a cloth soaked in white spirit.

4 Apply a coat of anti-rust primer, allow it to dry and apply one or two coats of an exterior-quality gloss paint suitable for metal. Allow each coat to dry before applying the next.

Light up your garden world

ADDING ORNAMENTAL LIGHTING

95

Don't use indoor fairy lights outside.

There's no point at all in creating a beautiful garden space if you can't use it after the sun goes down. Outdoor lighting can be both decorative and functional, creating a mood and adding to your sense of security and safety. Choose low-voltage systems, solar-powered lights or the more traditional candle-lit lanterns or garden torches — or a combination — to suit your needs. Solar-powered or electric lighting systems are convenient to use, but candles really add that romantic touch. A word of warning though about nocturnal alfresco entertaining — beware of insects! They love that flickering candle-light as much as you do. Be sure to have citronella candles or insect-repellent devices operating so you and your guests don't get eaten alive. Also, hang a few strings of exterior tree lights around the garden for that twinkly enchanted-grotto touch.

CANDLE-LIGHT IS SUBLIME ON A SUMMER EVENING BUT TAKE CARE, AN OPEN FLAME SHOULD NEVER BE LEFT UNATTENDED.

USE OUTDOOR LIGHTING TO ACCENT FEATURES IN THE GARDEN.

POSITIONING

☞ In general it's best to put outdoor lights where they'll be most effective or useful. If you have a pathway running through the garden, place little marker lights along the edges to illuminate your evening stroll. Outdoor dining areas always benefit from a few well-placed lights to enhance the mood — and to allow your dinner guests to see what they're eating! If you have a few fabulous plants, decorative garden structures or a water feature, then a subtle light will create a cool focal point in the garden during the hours of darkness or twilight.

LOW-VOLTAGE OUTDOOR LIGHTING

GET THAT AUTHENTIC GLOW!

☞ Low-voltage garden lighting kits contain all you'll need to install a small lighting system in your garden. Some can be expanded with extra lights, cables and connectors – refer to the manufacturer's guidelines for the maximum number of light units a single system will support. Extension devices are also available to increase the height of some globe and tier units. Because the voltage is low (12 volts), it means there is no need to dig deep trenches for the cables; a shallow layer of earth as a covering should be sufficient. All kits contain a transformer that steps household current down from the standard 240 volts to the required 12 volts.

Place the lights next to the intended sites, then run the cable between them, allowing a loop about 30 cm (12 in) long at each point for the connection.

Dig shallow trenches in which to bury the cables, then follow the manufacturer's instructions to connect each light to the cable. Now set the lights in place (most will have spikes to drive deep into the ground), bury the cable, then connect the system to the mains supply. (*See Warning box below.*)

WARNING

☞ Always follow the manufacturer's instructions. Don't take any risks where electricity is concerned and never tamper with or dismantle any electrical fittings or devices. It is advisable to connect the lighting system to the mains supply via an outdoor, weatherproof socket. The installation of such a device is definitely a job for a professional electrician. The rest you can easily do yourself.

Wall light

✺ JUST MAKE SURE THEY ALL SHINE ON YOUR BEST SIDE!

Tiered pedestal light

Globe pedestal light

Adjustable spotlight

Sizzle with style outdoors

BUILDING A BARBECUE

Build a brick barbecue in no time at all! This one is made from bricks stacked up in rows, one on top of the other — no messing around with mortar, either. The arrangement of bricks makes a really sturdy structure, but I would advise you not to build it much higher than the one shown. You can use any bricks you fancy, so long as they're all the same size. Light the charcoal and get cooking!

need

* Seventy-four bricks
* four paving slabs for the base
* brick bolster
* club hammer
* grill shelf from cooker
* steel sheet approx. 45 cm (18 in) square - ask a metal supplier to cut it for you

1 Put on your protective gloves. The paving slabs and bricks have rough edges and can cut or graze your skin quite badly if you're not careful. Lay the four paving slabs on a level surface to form the base for the barbecue. Take six bricks and lay them out in the pattern shown to form the first course. You can refer to the diagram given on page 185.

2 The second course is the same as the first, but rotated so that the bricks lie across the gaps in the first course. Lay the third as the first, and the fourth as the second. Alternate the rows in this way to build a tower of bricks ten courses high.

3 Now for the fire shelf. Take the steel sheet and lay it squarely on top of the tenth course. Lay another course of bricks, adding two half-bricks at the front. To cut a brick in half, place the blade of the brick bolster on the halfway point, then strike a few times with a club hammer. Then add another course like the first, but leave a gap at the front.

* WELL, I DON'T THINK IT'S CLEVER!

4 You can now install the grill shelf. Simply place it squarely on the brick tower, making sure that the corners overlap the bricks so that it's steady – you don't want your burgers to fall into the charcoal, do you? You can borrow a shelf from your cooker for barbecue use, then replace it when you're done.

✳ YOU KNOW WHAT THEY SAY — IF YOU CAN'T STAND THE HEAT, GET OUT OF THE KITCHEN! USE THE BARBECUE INSTEAD.

95 CLEAN IT UP

☞ Cleaning your greasy barbecue has to be done occasionally, so get your rubber gloves on! Buy some barbecue cleaner. This marvellous substance comes in an easy-to-use spray bottle and it will do most of the hard work for you. First remove any old ash or charcoal (make sure it's cold!), then place the part to be cleaned on some newspaper. Spray on the cleaner and leave it for about thirty minutes. By this time most of the greasy residue will have softened, so you can scrub it off using a stiff brush. Repeat the process for really burned-on remnants of food. Now wash the clean parts with soapy water and allow them to dry before reassembling the barbecue.

5 Now add a wind break. Use the same format as the previous course – you can build it a little higher if you choose (especially if it's windy). This row also holds the grill shelf in place. Finally, place one complete brick in the space in front of the fire shelf to act as a primitive air vent. If you need more air for the charcoal, simply take it out.

Hang 'em high

HANGING A BASKET

Hanging baskets that overflow with beautiful, fragrant flowers are a joy to behold in the summer months. If you are an avid gardener, you can plant your own basket with your favourite blooms. If, like me, you are a lazy gardener (and what's wrong with that?), you can buy some lovely ready-planted baskets from the local garden centre. Now all you have to do is mount secure wall brackets from which to suspend them.

need
* drill with masonry bit
* wall plugs
* hammer
* hanging bracket
* brass or rustproof screws
* screwdriver

1 Hold up the hanging bracket in the desired position and mark each screw hole. Use the drill and a masonry bit to make a hole at each position. If you need to use a ladder to get access to the area, make sure that the legs are in a safe position so that you don't fall off!

2 Next, insert a wall plug into each of the holes. The fit must be snug for the wall plug to be effective, so you may need to gently tap them in using a hammer. It is very important to use the recommended bit size for the wall plug.

3 If you buy a wall-mounted item in kit form, the manufacturer will usually provide suitable wall plugs and screws for installation. However, if the bracket is bought individually or you are remounting an old bracket, you will have to choose your own.

4 Make sure you have the screws in your pocket, then position the hanging bracket over the screw holes. Drive in one of the screws to hold the bracket loosely in place, then insert the other screws. When all the screws are in place, tighten them. You can now hang up your basket of plants with confidence and pride!

❋ I LIKE MY MEN LIKE MY BASKETS — SECURE AND READY FOR DISPLAY!

MAKING A PERGOLA

Pergolas give shade to a patio or create a covered archway in a garden. To construct a simple flat-top pergola is relatively easy. The framework consists of four corner posts joined by two side rails, which are spanned by cross rails. The cross rails are joined to the side rails by means of halving joints. With this type of joint, pieces of the same thickness are notched to half their thickness so they can interlock and are flush when joined.

need

* drill
* hammer and sledgehammer
* tenon saw and jigsaw
* try square and pencil
* chisel
* screwdriver
* eight coach screws
* four 75-mm (3-in)-square planed wooden posts (tall enough to stand under!)
* four 75-mm (3-in) metal fence-post spikes
* planed 10-cm x 5-cm (4-in x 2-in) timber for the two side rails and cross rails

❶ Mark the position of the pergola out on the ground, making sure the corners are all square. Drive the post spikes into the ground at each corner of the marked area using a sledgehammer (*see directions on page 146*). Cut the side rails and cross rails to length, about 30 cm (12 in) longer than the distance between the corner posts. Use a jigsaw to cut each end into a curved or sloping shape.

❷ Lay the side rails on the ground just outside the corner posts, and lay the cross rails in position. Mark the position of each halving joint along the top edge of each side rail. Mark the screw-hole positions.

IT'LL LOOK GREAT WHEN THE PLANTS GROW!

❸ Mark out each halving joint using a pencil and try square. Square down from each mark to the halfway point, then join the ends of the lines. Use a tenon saw to cut down to the cross mark, then chop out the waste using a chisel and hammer.

❹ Drill screw holes in the correct position through the side rails and the first and last cross rails. Secure the side rails to the corner posts using coach screws, then join the first and last cross rails to the side rails and screw them in position.

❺ Now take the remaining cross rails and simply slot them into position; the fit should be quite snug. You can screw them to the side rails from the top if you want more stability. Treat with preservative or stain to protect the wood from the weather.

How to keep your firewood dry

MAKING A LOG STORE

98

If you enjoy sitting cosily on the sofa in front of a roaring fire, you will know that having a plentiful supply of dry logs is a real advantage. This log store is easily constructed from tanalized rough-sawn timber. It has closed-in sides and a tarpaulin-covered lid and front flap. You can leave the timber in its natural state or stain it.

❶ The construction method is very simple: the diagram on page 185 shows how the pieces fit together. All you need to do before joining them together is drill a screw hole through each piece of wood. It's an easy process then to drive the screws home.

❷ Assemble four cross members to form the base of the log store. Try to space them out evenly, but you don't have to be too accurate about this. The pieces will keep the logs off the ground and allow air to circulate.

❸ Cut lengths of feather-edge board to fit across the back and sides. Beginning at the bottom of each section, nail each piece to the timber framework. Overlap the boards slightly to form a reasonably weatherproof outer layer. Remember to apply wood preservative, using a small brush, to all the cut ends of wood.

❹ For the lid, screw the remaining four pieces of wood together to form a rectangular frame – check at this point that the frame fits the top of the store – then nail on the plywood panel. Lay the lid upside-down on a large rectangle of tarpaulin and wrap the edges round the frame, folding corners neatly. Nail the tarpaulin to the framework.

❋ ONE SPARK FROM ME, SISTER, AND THE WHOLE LOT GOES UP IN SMOKE!

Dimensions

Basic pieces

You will need to cut the lengths of 50-mm x 50-mm (2-in x 2-in) timber, or you can ask the timber yard to do it

Log store

ten pieces, 90 cm (36 in) in length,
four pieces, 60 cm (24 in) in length

Lid

two pieces, 60 cm (24 in) in length
two pieces, 102.5 cm (41 in) in length
plywood rectangle, 72.5 cm x 102.5 cm
(29 in x 41 in)

5 Cut a rectangle of plastic tarpaulin to fit the front opening, allowing about 10 cm (4 in) extra at each short end. Cut a length of batten to fit the width of the rectangle. Wrap one short end round the batten and attach it with nails. The batten acts as a weight to keep the tarpaulin flap from blowing around in the wind, keeping out the weather and keeping the logs dry.

6 Nail the free top edge of the tarpaulin flap along the uppermost front cross member of the log store. Now place the covered lid in position. Your log store should now be pretty weatherproof; just lift up the flap to reach the logs inside the store.

✳ KEEP YOUR LOGS COSY AND THEY'LL DO THE SAME FOR YOU!

need

✳ 50-mm x 50-mm (2-in x 2-in) tanalized rough-sawn timber
✳ length of thin wooden batten
✳ drill
✳ 75-mm (3-in) screws
✳ screwdriver
✳ saw
✳ sheet of plywood
✳ 25-mm (1-in) nails
✳ feather-edge boards
✳ hammer
✳ sheet of plastic tarpaulin
✳ wood preservative and brush

A Gaudi-esque mosaic garden stool

99

AS I'VE said before, concrete is an amazing substance (I really can't get enough of it!), and you can use it in small quantities to create decorative or functional garden structures. For this garden stool, I've used tubular metal frames from old stools as the basic skeleton, or armature, for these garden seats/plant stands. Simply pad the frame with polystyrene, wrap it in chicken wire, secure it with galvanized wire and apply a couple of layers of concrete over the top. When the whole thing is dry you can apply a mosaic decoration in the pattern and colour scheme of your choice.

✳ GIVE ME SOMETHING HOT AND SPANISH ANY TIME!

1 Remove the seat from the old stool. Using a sharp kitchen knife, cut two curved, roughly square shapes from the polystyrene sheet to form the seat. Wire it to the centre of the tubular frame. Turn the frame upside-down and press a polystyrene ball on to the end of each leg. Turn right-side up.

2 Put on your gloves and use side cutters or tin snips to cut a large square of chicken wire. Wrap the wire over the seat and squeeze the corners down and around the legs. Use the thin galvanized wire to hold the mesh in place. Turn the frame upside-down.

3 Cut four pieces of mesh about 40 cm x 25 cm (16 in x 10 in), and wrap these around the legs, covering the polystyrene balls. Squeeze the wire mesh tightly around the chair legs and the balls to follow the shape closely.

4 Pour a small quantity of concrete mix into an old bucket. Add water and mix, carefully following the instructions provided on the bag. Do not overwater the mixture because this will result in weak concrete.

5 Put on a pair of latex gloves and use your hands to spread a thin layer of the concrete mixture over the entire armature. It's a good idea to put the armature on a plastic sheet to catch any blobs. Set the concreted piece aside for a day or so to allow the concrete to set, then repeat the process, right-side up.

✳ IT'S NOT OFTEN YOU GET A CHANCE TO SIT ON YOUR ASSETS!

6 Use tile nippers to cut the coloured ceramic tiles into small irregular shapes, then use a knife to apply tile adhesive to the back of each shape. This process is known as 'buttering' – you can use an ordinary household knife to do this. Press the tile into position, following an ordered pattern or just randomly to make a free-form design. You could also put a few glass nuggets here and there to add interest.

7 When the adhesive is dry you will need to fill in all the gaps between the tiles. This is called 'grouting'. Apply the grout using a small spatula, pressing the grout into all the gaps and scraping off any excess at the same time. Wipe over the grouted surface with a wet cloth to finish. When the grouting is dry you can polish the tiles to remove any powdery deposits.

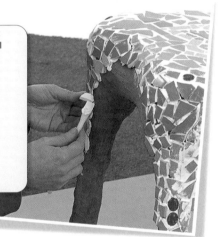

need

* tubular metal stool
* thick polystyrene sheet
* sharp kitchen knife
* thin galvanized wire
* chicken wire
* side cutters or tin snips
* four tennis-ball-sized polystyrene spheres
* ready-mix dry concrete

* old bucket
* piece of board (to mix on)
* work gloves
* latex gloves
* coloured ceramic tiles
* tile nippers
* glass nuggets
* waterproof tile adhesive/grout
* cloth or sponge
* old butter knife

Tinkle, tinkle, little spa

MAKING A SIMPLE WATER FEATURE

100

There's nothing more soothing to the ear than the gentle sound of bubbling water — a small, well-situated water feature makes a fabulous focal point in the garden. Get yourself to the garden centre and choose a kit from the many varieties available. Most kits will include everything you need (except decorative details such as pebbles), plus instructions for installation. This one features a pump with a telescopic fountain so you can vary the height of the water jet. Now all you need to do is choose a site and dig a hole!

✳ WHAT? I'VE BEEN HERE FOR HOURS AND THERE'S NO FISH IN THERE?

1 The kit will include a container and a submersible water pump, plus fittings. Choose the site carefully. It needs to be pretty level to avoid too much excavation work.

2 Dig a hole that is large enough to accommodate the plastic container. You can also add a layer of damp sand in the bottom of the hole if you wish.

3 Drop the container into the hole. If it does not fit well, then take it out and dig out some more soil.

4 When you are satisfied with the fit of the container, make a final check using a spirit level – it's important that the container rim is perfectly level. Pack any gaps around the edge of the container with soil.

5 Follow the instructions for fitting the water pump with the required telescopic fountain attachments, then place the unit inside the plastic container. Fill with water up to the recommended level, then close the flaps.

172

LANDSCAPING YOUR WATER FEATURE

☞ Once you have installed your wonderful water feature, create a natural look by landscaping the surrounding area afterwards. Use some fresh turf cut to shape or make an arrangement of bricks or larger stones as a decorative edge. Pebbles and gravel are effective, but don't overdo it, because the arrangement should look attractive once the water has been turned off! A variety of small plants placed between the pebbles or miniature alpines planted in gravel will also create an attractive focal point. With a little luck the water feature will attract wildlife, too.

A WATER FEATURE CREATES A SPECIAL PLACE IN THE GARDEN.

EXCITE THE SENSES WITH THE SOUND OF TRICKLING WATER.

6 Wash all the pebbles in a bucket of water to remove dust and dirt. Once the feature is assembled, you can pile the pebbles on top of it, then turn on the pump and watch the water bubbling through. Rearrange the pebbles if necessary to make an even flow.

Decorate the surrounding area with turf or bricks.

need
* water-feature kit
* shovel
* sand
* spirit level
* pebbles

PUMP CABLE

☞ What to do with the pump cable? You'll need to run it unobtrusively from the feature to a power point. If you do not need to have the pump on all the time, then you can easily connect it to an indoor socket. Simply plug in the feature to enjoy while sitting outdoors! If you would like the water feature to have constant running water, you'll have to bury the cables in shallow trenches running from the feature to a weatherproof external socket. This means that you can keep it running all the time, or have it linked to a timer. Remember: if you don't have an outdoor socket, ask an electrician to install one for you! Dealing with mains electricity is a job for the professionals.

OUTSIDE HELP

Now, what do you do when you do need a man and how do you know if you need one or not?

Calling in the big boys

We've had 100 things you don't need a man for in the garden. Now you need to recognize when an outside job is too big or dangerous for you and when it's time to call in the experts — we're talking major electrical jobs, roof repairs and anything involving heavy machinery, girls. Before you start dealing with contractors, make sure you understand the problem, know the jargon and have a good idea of exactly what you want done. Then all you need to do is be a demon at negotiating a fair price and a sensible schedule.

✳ WHO NEEDS
A MAN...I'M
QUITE HAPPY
HANDLING
LARGE
EQUIPMENT!

TO DO OR NOT TO DO?

That's the question! If you're wondering about tackling an exterior maintenance project, then the first thing to consider is scale. Exterior DIY tasks are slightly different from the interior jobs because there are more extremes involved. For example, a roof can be very HIGH, pavers can be very HEAVY and outdoor wiring can be very DANGEROUS. If you have a knee-trembling fear of heights, then roof repairs are out of the question.

Don't try to lay a patio using huge paving slabs. Compromise: use smaller, easily manageable paving stones that won't break your back.

My approach is more often than not budget-driven; you don't want to spend a fortune contracting someone to do a job you could easily do yourself. But, on the other hand, why kill yourself for the sake of a small fee? For example, you've bought slabs and sand for the patio, but do you want to do three or four trips to and from the DIY store in your car? Why not pay for delivery — for a few pounds you can save yourself a lot of time and effort. While we're talking deliveries, 'to your door' may be exactly that — the door. If the intended patio area is at the bottom of the garden it's always worth asking the delivery person to take the goods to the site — smile nicely and tip well!

For the purposes of 'not doing it', I've split large, pay-the-man-to-do tasks into three categories: the High, the Low and the Dangerous. Look at the lists when you feel a big project coming on or have an important repair to do, then examine your bank balance, grit your teeth and get on the phone!

THE HIGH

In this category I have placed any jobs that involve climbing up a ladder. Extensive roof repairs or replacements are definitely jobs for the big boys — they know what they're doing and will have all the right access equipment and skills to match. Window cleaners also have skills involving access equipment and chamois leathers. Don't risk life and limb cleaning upstairs windows if they're a bit high — just pay the man. Also, window replacements and reglazing large windows are definitely a DIY don't. Last but not least — trees. Felling large trees is not a job for the untrained. Also, mature trees can affect the foundations on which your house is built. Never fell a tree close to your building without the advice of a tree surgeon, or, better still, get them to do it for you.

THE LOW

As for the low-down and dirty ground-level (and below) tasks, this includes all work involving major drainage systems or serious blockages in sewage pipes, damp-proofing or repairs to damp-proof courses. The foundations that your house sits on are pretty important; if you think you have a problem in that department, ask a professional for advice. If you're considering resurfacing a driveway or replacing a concrete basement floor, then get the men with the big concrete mixers to do it for you. Small amounts of this stuff are manageable, but there's no joy in having to lug and mix huge quantities of it. Any substantial bricks-and-mortar activity like constructing an extension, a garage or a shed for storage requires the skill of a trained craftsman. While a small patio is an achievable goal, a huge paved area may prove too much to handle. The same is true of major excavation work. If you have a big sloping garden to level, hire a man with the right machinery to move the earth for you!

THE DANGEROUS

This covers anything to do with the mains power or water supply. Dig trenches yourself, but any connections, modifications or repairs to any major service supply should be carried out by a qualified person. All major wiring jobs, such as running permanent power cables to sheds, sophisticated security devices and systems or automatic garage-door openers, should always be carried out by recommended technicians. These are expensive and really need to be dealt with by an expert.

SO GET ONE IF...

☞ extensive roof repairs or replacements are needed.

☞ large windows need replacing and reglazing.

☞ mature trees need felling.

☞ there are major blockages in drainage systems or sewage pipes.

☞ a damp-proof course is needed.

☞ resurfacing an entire floor or driveway is needed.

☞ major modifications or repair to the water supply are needed.

☞ a large expanse of land needs levelling.

☞ major electrical wiring jobs need doing – especially those involving water at the same time, such as the timer for the sprinkler system or a waterproof outdoor electrical socket.

LET ME DO THE HEAVY DANGEROUS STUFF!

HE'S YOUR KNIGHT IN SHINING ARMOUR!

HOW TO GET A MAN IN

Finding the right man may be a problem if you don't know how and where to look. A reliable, skilled contractor is a real find. Ask anyone who's ever engaged the services of a professional. Your first avenue of investigation should be your friends — a personal recommendation is better than any reference written on paper. Just put the word out that you're looking, then wait to see what happens. The Yellow Pages can be a good source of information. Jot down some names, then make some enquiries. However, before you speak to anyone directly, be sure to make a list of crucial questions to ask. Can he do the job? When can he do the job? How much will he charge for the job? Can he give you a written estimate? Will he guarantee the work? Also, make sure you know exactly what you need doing. Be specific — it'll save time in the long run. Do a bit of research, familiarize yourself with the terminology and learn correct names for things so you won't be umm-ing and ahh-ing on the phone. It's a clear signal to an unscrupulous contractor that you don't know what you're talking about and you can be completely taken for a ride. Don't fall into that trap!

So you've compiled a shortlist, what next? Well, the cheapest may not be the best. Then again, the most expensive may not be the best, either — so the one offering a mid-priced estimate is probably a good choice.

＊ HE'S GORGEOUS, BUT I WON'T LET HIM KNOW UNTIL THE JOB'S FINISHED!

CHECK OUT THE GOODS THOROUGHLY BEFORE PAYING, LADIES!

Finally, check any qualifications. If your chosen man says he belongs to a certain association or has any fancy letters after his name, it's a good idea that you make sure that they're genuine before you shake hands and clinch the deal!

AND WHEN HE'S IN

Well done, you've hired your man! It's a good idea to confirm this in writing just as a safeguard. If it's a fairly substantial job, then ask him to draw up a contract giving the job description and any terms of agreement. That way both parties know exactly where they stand and have a piece of paper to wave if things go wrong (and he can do the waving too if you don't keep your part of the deal!). The contract should include a payment schedule, which you both agree to before work starts. You may be required to put some money up front to pay for materials and so on, or split the agreed fee into portions, payable when a certain amount of work has been completed to your satisfaction.

At this point, double-check that you're both speaking the same language. That is, try to supply him with all the information that he may need: words and pictures, plans, colour swatches and material samples, to make sure there are no mistakes or misunderstandings. After all, he's being paid to do a job, not to be a mind reader, and if he's badly or ambiguously briefed, then it really isn't his fault. If there's any change to the original plan, however small, then make sure he knows that he should consult you first.

KEEPING IT RUNNING SMOOTHLY

When any decorating, maintenance or installation procedure is under way, you can be sure that a certain amount of dirt will follow. Don't despair, this is normal, even if you do it yourself, but you can make life easy for yourself (and your workman). If, for example, there is no side access to the garden, cover areas indoors with plastic tarpaulins or dust sheets — you don't want a muddy trail through your house, and the poor man doesn't want to have to worry about tiptoeing down your hallway either. Also, make sure that he's familiar with everything he may need access to and that he has your contact number if a problem arises and you need to be consulted. Be flexible, too. There are many things that are beyond anyone's control, so don't lose your cool if a mishap or delay occurs that really isn't anyone's fault. So long as you maintain good communication channels with your workman, there shouldn't be any problems.

Another important point to mention before you begin major, messy or noisy jobs, either by yourself or using a contractor, is to speak to your neighbours. Let them know what you intend to do and when, then agree to acceptable 'noise-making' hours. It pays to stay on good terms with the folks next door.

OK. He has his instructions, he knows what he's doing, you're happy, he's happy — now make sure that you have plenty of tea and biscuits to keep him going and leave him alone to get down to it!

ANATOMY LESSONS
GETTING DOWN TO IT

A wonderful specimen — ready, willing and able! Congratulate yourself on choosing the best man for the job. Keep him well fed with tea and biscuits, and you'll not be disappointed. If he proves really good, get a handful of his business cards and give them to neighbours and friends — contractors rely on their good reputation.

NOT QUITE SURE WHAT I'M SUPPOSED TO BE DOING HERE, BUT IF I STAND HERE LONG ENOUGH, PERHAPS I'LL GET A CUP OF TEA...

TOUSLED HAIR
(he hasn't got time to wash it)

FIRM GRIP
(preferably with loads of calluses – he's a hard worker)

BARE CHEST
(shirt off – means he's working hard)

NOT EXACTLY A SIX-PACK
(well, we don't mind if he enjoys a beer or two, so long as it's not on the job!!)

STRONG, MUSCULAR ARMS
(now that's what we like to see, girls!)

Garden repair record

USE THIS check-list as a handy reminder of what to do, where to do it and when to do it — and also to keep track of when you did it last. Make sure you don't do more work than necessary, girls! Keep all your notes in a safe place so that you can easily refer to them when the time comes for regular maintenance procedures or an emergency arises.

WHAT AND WHEN?

Make dated notes of monthly and annual checks and routine maintenance — prevention is always better than cure.

DRAINS	ROOF AND GUTTERS	WINDOWS AND DOORS	SECURITY SYSTEMS	EXTERIOR DECORATION
			Change batteries if cordless	

WATER FEATURE PUMP/ SPRINKLER SYSTEM	GARAGE-DOOR OPENING MECHANISM	BULB PLANTING	GATES AND FENCES	COMPOST
		What and where		When started, when to turn

WHO

Keep a record of work, repairs or replacements done — and keep any receipts or guarantees. Most guarantees are transferable to a new owner if you sell your house. You need names, phone numbers and dates, for example.

KEEP SAFE

Keep important documents such as operation manuals, receipts and guarantees for equipment or works carried out. Garden plans, sprinkler-system routes, notes on quantities and materials, paint-colour codes and suppliers, etc., could all be useful at a later date when the time comes for a simple repair.

DAMP-PROOF COURSE	ROOF REPAIRS/ REPLACEMENTS	WINDOW REPLACEMENTS/ REPAIRS	SECURITY/ SPRINKLER- SYSTEM INSTALLATION	BUILDING WORK

DRAINAGE	BUILDING WORK	GARDEN- EQUIPMENT SERVICE/ REPAIR	OUTDOOR ELECTRICAL SOCKETS	TREE REMOVAL/ TREATMENT

A girl can always use a little guidance

TEMPLATES

Here are scaled-down templates, patterns and constructional diagrams to help you complete all the creative projects in this book.

☛ Cut out two fronts and two sides, then construct the bird table using wood glue, nails and battens cut to size as shown.

FRONT

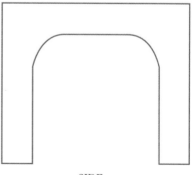

SIDE

Making a bird table, pages 106–107

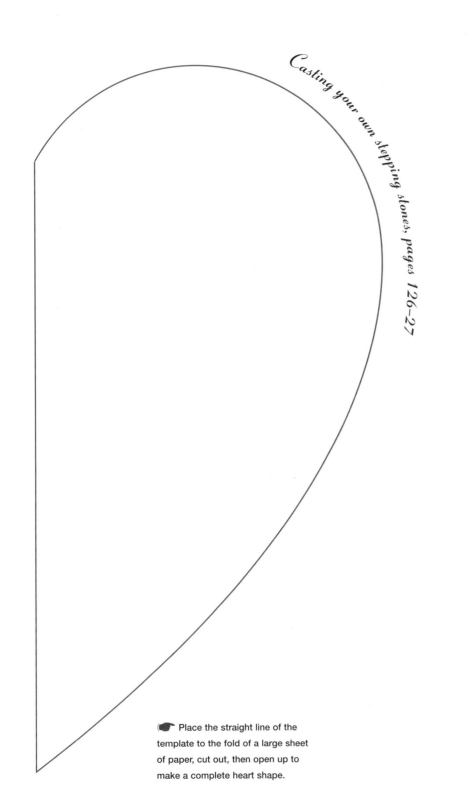

Casting your own stepping stones, pages 126–27

 Place the straight line of the template to the fold of a large sheet of paper, cut out, then open up to make a complete heart shape.

 Mark eight eyelet positions with pencil crosses. Each should be 38 mm (1½ in) away from the fold lines and 10 cm (4 in) in from the edge.

Making a hammock, pages 158–59

183

Making an art deco-style trellis, pages 152–53

☛ Cut all the pieces of wood to size as indicated on page 153, then construct as shown in the diagram below.

UNDERSIDE

Repairing a garden parasol page 156

TOP

Building a barbecue, pages 164–65

☞ Build up the brick tower using the course diagrams as a guide. The structure will be quite sturdy and needs no mortar.

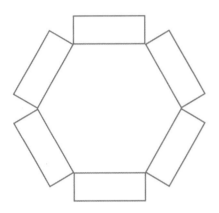

FIRST COURSE

Making a log store, pages 168–69

☞ Cut the rough-sawn wood pieces to the size indicated on page 169. Then simply drill screw holes and fix the log store together following the constructional diagram below.

SECOND COURSE

◀— 90 cm (3 ft) —▶

GLOSSARY OF TERMS

AGGREGATES The term for materials (fine or coarse) that are added to a cement mix, such as sand, gravel or larger stone.

ALGAE Simple, non-flowering plants without roots, leaves or stems, for example, seaweed, lichen and moss.

ANGLE GRINDER An electrically powered tool with a heavy-duty revolving blade for cutting brick, metal and stone.

ARMATURE The framework around which a structure is moulded.

AUGER A long, flexible rod used to clear blockages from water and waste pipes.

BALLAST A mixture of sand and crushed stone for mixing with cement to make concrete. Also known as combined aggregate.

BATTEN A narrow strip of wood.

BEVEL A slanting or sloping edge.

BIB TAP An outdoor tap.

BIT A metal attachment for a drill to facilitate drilling holes of various diameter.

BRADAWL A small hand tool with a pointed spike, used to make pilot holes in wood.

BRICK BOLSTER A chisel with a wide blade for cutting bricks and pavers.

BUTT A joint between two pieces of wood. The pieces are cut square and one is butted to its neighbour. *Also:* Showcase body part that keeps its fine form with diligent home and garden maintenance.

BUTTERING The application of tile adhesive with a small knife.

CHALK LINE A tool for marking straight lines *(see page 11)*.

CLADDING Interlocking or overlapping boards made of UPVC, aluminium or wood that cover the exterior walls of a building.

CLEARANCE HOLE A hole drilled into sheet material to facilitate easy insertion of a jigsaw blade, or a small-diameter hole used as guide for a screw.

CLEAT A T-shaped or similar projection that is used to secure a rope *(see page 100)*.

CLOSEBOARD FENCING Fencing made from overlapping feather-edge boards nailed on to horizontal wooden rails.

CLUB HAMMER A heavy hammer for use in cutting paving slabs, or other heavy work.

COACH SCREW These screws have a square head and are driven into the work using a spanner. Used for heavy-duty construction.

COLD CHISEL A narrow chisel used in conjunction with a hammer to cut paving slabs, metal, etc.

CROSS-HEAD The term for screws with a cross-shaped indentation in the head, for use with cross-head (Pozidrive or Phillips) screwdrivers.

CROSS-RAIL A horizontal wooden rail to which fence boards are attached.

DAMP-PROOF COURSE A layer of impervious material that is used to keep moisture from rising up into walls.

DRAIN RODS Flexible rods that join together for use in clearing a blocked drain.

DRY-LAYING Laying a patio or path without using mortar.

DUAL-PURPOSE LADDER A ladder that can be used as a stepladder or as an extending ladder.

EAVES The part of a roof that meets or overhangs the walls of a building.

EDGING TOOL A tool with a sharp, semi-circular blade used for trimming lawn edges.

EFFLORESCENCE A white powdery substance that forms on brick or mortar walls as a result of salts migrating to the surface.

FEATHER-EDGE BOARDS Wooden boards that have one thick edge and one thin one, enabling them to be overlapped when used in fencing or cladding.

FINIAL A diamond-shaped piece of wood placed at the roof apex of a small building, or a decorative ornament at the top, end or corner of an object.

FLASHING Metal strips (usually lead, zinc or mortar fillet) used to weatherproof the gaps between roofing surfaces.

FLAT-HEAD A screwdriver designed for use with slotted screws.

FLUSH When two surfaces are perfectly level with each other. *Also:* Skin condition associated with getting a gorgeous contractor on the job (*see STUD*).

FOOTING A concrete support that is sunk into the ground and used to support a decking framework.

FORMWORK Temporary wooden framework used as a guide and containment when laying a patio or path.

FRENCHMAN A hand tool used to scoop up excess mortar. *Also:* A charming language barrier worth having around the home and garden.

FROG A depression commonly found on one side of a brick that acts as a key for mortar. *Also:* Web-footed garden amphibian that can be kissed to reveal handsome prince.

GALVANIZED Covered with a protective layer of zinc. Objects manufactured from galvanized iron or steel are less prone to rust.

GLAZING SPRIGS Small nails used to secure a glazed pane into a window frame.

GRAIN The direction or pattern of wood fibres.

GROUT Used to fill and seal gaps between tiles after they have been attached to walls.

I DIDN'T KNOW THAT LOG STORES CAME IN A KIT!

HALVING JOINT A wood joint that makes use of slots cut into pieces of wood (*see page 167*).

HASP AND STAPLE A device used in conjunction with a padlock to secure a door.

HEAVE The opposite of *SUBSIDENCE*. *Also:* Your least favourite verb, so take heed of protective clothing and equipment warnings when working with chemicals (*see page 69*).

HYDRAULIC GUILLOTINE A device for cutting paving slabs (*see page 16*).

JOIST A horizontal or metal supporting beam for walls, ceilings or floors.

KEY The term referring to a surface that has been sanded ready for painting or gluing.

LADDER STAY A wooden batten-and-peg device that enables you to secure a ladder in a safe position (*see page 19*).

LANDSCAPING MATERIAL Fabric used in external construction work. It allows water to drain down to the earth beneath, but does not allow weeds or other organic material to penetrate upwards.

LOPPER Giant secateurs with long handles used for trimming trees and undergrowth.

MASKING TAPE Self-adhesive paper tape used to mask off areas when painting.

MITRE Joint between two pieces of wood where the ends of each piece have been cut to the same angle.

MORTAR Building material (a fine mixture of cement, lime and sand) used to bond bricks and other masonry parts.

MULCH A mixture of leaves, bark or compost material.

PALING A pointed, wooden stake used in picket fencing.

PAVER A paving brick.

PEGBOARD Hardboard covered with a regular pattern of small round holes.

PERGOLA An arched structure in a garden that provides a framework for climbing or trailing plants.

PIR MOTION SENSOR PIR is an abbreviation for 'passive infra-red'. PIR motion sensors are used in conjunction with outdoor security lights; they detect movement within a given area, causing the lights to be switched on.

PLATE VIBRATOR An electrically powered flattening tool for use in landscaping projects (*see page 16*).

PLUGGING CHISEL A tool for removing loose mortar between bricks (*see page 14*).

PLUMB LINE A device for finding true vertical lines (*see page 15*).

POINTING The shaping of mortar joints between bricks (*see pages 70–71*).

PTFE TAPE Waterproof tape that is used in plumbing in order to make watertight seals in pipe fittings.

PUTTY KNIFE A knife for applying and shaping filler (*see page 14*).

RCD Residual current device. A circuit-breaking safety device designed to provide protection from electric shock.

REBATE A rectangular recess found along the edge of a frame or moulded workpiece.

RISER The vertical portion of a step.

RISING MAIN The name given to the first section of water pipe in a domestic plumbing system. It usually enters the house under the kitchen sink and follows the wall upwards.

WHAT DO YOU MEAN ALISON JENKINS TELLS IT BETTER THAN I DO?

SLEDGEHAMMER A long-handled heavy hammer for driving in fence-post spikes and breaking up old masonry.

SOLE PLATES Timber laid on concrete footings across a decking site to support the joists and deck construction.

SPINDLE The rod or pin around which a door handle revolves.

SPLINING TOOL A screen-installation tool (see page 82).

STOP VALVE A valve that is inserted into the mains water pipe in order to control water flow.

STRAINING WIRE/WINDING BRACKET Mechanism used to keep the mesh of a wire fence taut and secure.

STRIMMER An electrically powered tool for neatening lawn edges along paths or around irregular objects, such as trees.

STRING A shaped side panel that supports stair treads.

STUD Vertical timber which forms part of a stud partition wall. *Also*: More abundant in the path of us do-it-yourselfers, found in key supply stops, such as B&Q and the like. Worth the work!

SUBSIDENCE The gradual caving in or sinking of an area of ground.

TAMPING A method for levelling and compacting loose earth or other substances (see page 117).

TANALIZED TIMBER Wood for outdoor use that has been specially treated with preservatives.

THRESHOLD A piece of wood attached permanently across the entrance to a door. *Also*: Prime entrances over which truly romantic STUDS carry us hard-working girls at the end of a hard day's work.

TIN SNIPS A tool for cutting metal and UPVC materials. Particularly useful for roofing jobs (see page 14).

TINE A prong or sharp point, such as on a garden fork.

TREAD The horizontal part of a step.

TRELLIS An ornamental latticework frame used as a support for climbing plants or as a dividing screen in a garden.

TRY SQUARE A tool used as a guide to mark square corners before cutting (see page 15). *Also*: At times, far more reliable than the STUD or that stunning FRENCHMAN.

VOLATILE ORGANIC COMPOUND A chemical compound that participates in photo-chemical reactions. Such compounds are associated with poor air quality and the production of carcinogens.

WALL PLUG Plastic sleeve used to encase a screw. The wall plug is inserted into a drilled hole in a masonry or brick wall. When the screw is inserted, the plug expands to form a firm gripping surface for the screw's thread.

WASHER Rubber disc found in a tap.

WEATHERBOARD A moulded strip of wood attached across the bottom of an inward-opening external door.

WIRE WOOL Fine metal fibres gathered together to form a pad used for sanding.

FURTHER READING

100 THINGS YOU DON'T NEED A MAN FOR!

Alison Jenkins (Aurum Press, 2001)

BUILD YOUR OWN PATHS, STEPS AND PATIOS

Penny Swift, Janek Szymanowski
(New Holland, 2001)

COLLINS DIY GUIDE: OUTDOORS AND GARDENS

Albert Jackson, David Day
(Collins, 1993)

THE COMPLETE BOOK OF STEP-BY-STEP OUTDOOR DIY

Mike Lawrence, Penny Swift and Janek Szymanowski (Sterling, 2001)

DECKS AND PATIOS FOR DUMMIES

Robert Beckstrom
(John Wiley & Sons Inc., 1998)

DO IT YOURSELF: OUTDOOR PROJECTS

Jonathan Edwards (Southwater, 2002)

EXTERIOR HOME REPAIRS & IMPROVEMENTS (BLACK & DECKER HOME IMPROVEMENT LIBRARY)

(Creative Publishing International, 1995)

FENCES, WALLS & GATES

Jerry Ferris, Tim Himsel
(Creative Publishing International, 2001)

MAKING PATHS AND WALKWAYS

Paige Gilchrist Blomgren (Lark Books, 2001)

OUTDOOR REPAIRS (DO-IT-YOURSELF ESSENTIALS)

David Holloway (Southwater, 2002))

OUTDOOR WATER FEATURES: 16 EASY-TO-BUILD PROJECTS FOR YOUR YARD AND GARDEN

Alan Bridgewater and Gill Bridgewater
(Storey Books, 2001)

READER'S DIGEST COMPLETE DIY MANUAL

(Reader's Digest, 1998)

ROOFING AND INSULATION

Mike Lawrence
(The Crowood Press, 2001)

ROOFING AND SIDING

Lynne Gilberg (Sunset Books, 2000)

SHEDS: THE DO-IT-YOURSELF GUIDE FOR BACKYARD BUILDERS

David Stiles (Firefly Books, 1998)

USEFUL WEBSITES/ SUPPLIERS

B&Q
www.diy.com

DIG-IT.CO.UK
Online garden centre
www.dig-it.co.uk

DIY FIXIT
www.diyfixit.co.uk

FOCUS
www.focusdiy.co.uk

HOMEBASE
www.homebase.co.uk

SCREWFIX
www.screwfix.com

WICKES
www.wickes.co.uk

Index

DON'T MIND ME, I'M NOT EVEN IN THE INDEX!

Acknowledgements

AUTHOR ACKNOWLEDGEMENTS

I'd like to dedicate this book to my Mam and Dad, Adrian, Daisy and William, M&M, Helen, David and Keryl, and all the other lovely people I am so lucky to have as friends and family. Thanks to Caroline for support, services rendered and loan of nodding cat. Many, many thanks to Clare for bed & breakfast, girlie solidarity and positive reinforcement! Last but not least, a great big thank you to all at The Ivy Press and the studio for all the hard work, perseverance and encouragement — we got there in the end!

☛ The author and publisher would like to thank the following for their assistance and for the loan of props:

Black and Decker (all power tools)

Bluebell, Brighton

Cissy Mo, Brighton

Focus Do-It All (garden shed)

Harris (paintbrushes)

Hozelock (water feature hose and attachments, garden lights)

HSS Hire shops (rental equipment)

International Paints (floor paint, vinyl paint, metal paint)

Jaymart (artificial grass)

Kitschen Sync., London

Ronseal (wood stains and decking sealants and treatments)

South Coast Roofing Supplies (roof tiles)

Stanley (hand tools)

Toolbank (hand tools, toolbelt, toolbox)

✳ I'D LIKE TO THANK MY AGENT, MY STYLIST, MY HAIR GURU, MY SCRIPT EDITOR, MY NAIL ARTIST, MY MUM, MY DOG, MY CAT...